Flash Programming for the Social & Behavioral Sciences

MW00914487

Flash Programming for the Social & Behavioral Sciences

A Simple Guide to Sophisticated Online Surveys and Experiments

Yana Weinstein
Washington University in St. Louis

With contributions by K. Andrew DeSoto

Los Angeles | London | New Delhi
Singapore | Washington DC

Los Angeles | London | New Delhi
Singapore | Washington DC

FOR INFORMATION:

SAGE Publications, Inc.

2455 Teller Road

Thousand Oaks, California 91320

E-mail: order@sagepub.com

SAGE Publications Ltd.

1 Oliver's Yard

55 City Road

London EC1Y 1SP

United Kingdom

SAGE Publications India Pvt. Ltd.

B 1/I 1 Mohan Cooperative Industrial Area

Mathura Road, New Delhi 110 044

India

SAGE Publications Asia-Pacific Pte. Ltd.

3 Church Street

#10-04 Samsung Hub

Singapore 049483

Acquisitions Editor: Vicki Knight

Associate Editor: Lauren Habib

Editorial Assistant: Kalie Koscielak

Production Editor: Laura Stewart

Copy Editor: Tina Hardy

Typesetter: C&M Digitals, Ltd.

Proofreader: Jennifer Thompson

Indexer: Judy Hunt

Cover Designer: Anupama Krishan

Marketing Manager: Helen Salmon

Permissions Editor: Adele Hutchinson

Copyright © 2013 by SAGE Publications, Inc.

Printed in the United States of America

Library of Congress Cataloging-in-Publication Data

Weinstein, Yana.

Flash programming for the social & behavioral sciences: a simple guide to sophisticated online surveys and experiments / Yana Weinstein ; with contributions from K. Andrew DeSoto.

p. cm.
Includes bibliographical references and index.

ISBN 978-1-4129-9635-8 (pbk.)

1. Flash (Computer file) 2. Web sites--Authoring programs. 3. Internet surveys—Software. I. DeSoto, K. Andrew. II. Title.

TR897.7.W4495 2013
006.6'960243—dc23   2012002533

This book is printed on acid-free paper.

12 13 14 15 16 10 9 8 7 6 5 4 3 2 1

For Asya and Leva Tcherniak

TABLE OF CONTENTS

ABOUT THE AUTHOR

 Dr. Yana Weinstein is a psychology researcher and data analyst at Washington University in St. Louis, Missouri. She received her PhD in cognitive psychology from University College London. She divides her time among human memory research, data analysis for academic and commercial projects, and encouraging psychologists to use the latest technology for their research.

PREFACE

When I secured my place in graduate school, I went to meet my future adviser to find out what topics I should read up on over the summer. I was expecting a lengthy reading list, but instead I got one simple instruction: Learn to program. Most experimental psychology labs have a preferred programming language for their experiments and all new lab members are expected to learn it and become proficient programmers. Somewhat surprisingly, however, programming is seldom explicitly taught, and resources for self-instruction are scarce or not specifically tailored to psychologists. That summer, I hunted unsuccessfully for the ideal textbook—one that would teach me the basics of the language, bypass all the functionality I wouldn't need, and cut straight through to the techniques required for programming psychology experiments. Of course there was no such textbook, so I muddled through with endless online searches and adapting code from more advanced students while acquiring all their bad habits. In writing this book, I compiled all the information I was unable to find, ranging from specifics such as "How do I present stimuli in a random order?" to bigger questions such as "How do I collect data online?" in a format that is most intuitive to social and behavioral scientists—one in which each new technique is introduced in the context of a common aspect of survey or experiment design.

ACKNOWLEDGMENTS

My greatest thanks for making this book happen go to Decision Technology Ltd. (Dectech), Kathleen McDermott and Roddy Roediger, Vicki Knight, and Andy DeSoto. I would never have thought of learning Flash had I not seen it put to work by the staff at Dectech, who run huge online surveys and experiments and collect data in a fraction of the time it used to take me in the lab. As a casual data analyst on various projects with Dectech, I was not involved in programming the experiments in Flash (they have dedicated programmers for this), but I was very curious to learn, and I ended up doing so in my spare time.

When Kathleen McDermott and Roddy Roediger (my postdoctoral advisers at the time) became aware of the possibilities of rapid online data collection, they allowed me to try out a few of our studies with this method. One thing led to another, and soon I was teaching Flash programming to psychology graduate students in the department—but Kathleen took it one step further and encouraged me to put all the information from the class (and more) into a textbook format. Kathleen took the time to chat with Vicki Knight on my behalf, and a great collaboration was born. This book would never have been published without Kathleen's initiative and support. Vicki was extremely enthusiastic about the project from the start, and she has been a great pleasure to work with (it was especially lovely to have a British expat connection). I would also like to thank the reviewers: Nathan D. Martin, Michelle C. Bligh, Melissa Birkett, and Jennifer L. Callahan for their insightful comments on an earlier draft of this book, which undoubtedly made it a much better finished product.

Finally, Andy DeSoto participated in the creation of the book every step of the way: He read every single word, corrected awkward sentences and mislabeled concepts, rewrote whole paragraphs, and verified all the code samples. Andy is a PhD student and human memory researcher at Washington University in St. Louis, and he got involved in the project after taking my Flash class. You can visit his personal website at http://me.andydesoto.com/ or follow him on Twitter at @kadesoto.

WHY FLASH?

Adobe Flash is currently one of the most popular languages for animated web content, and almost all modern computers are capable of playing Flash content. Psychologists have recently started to take advantage of this to collect experimental data online. Flash is used not only for questionnaire-based studies but also for sophisticated experiments involving stimuli such as pictures, dynamic shapes, and animation. This language arguably offers the most flexibility to social and behavioral scientists: It allows absolute control over design and visual aspects and only requires simple online implementation. Accurate reaction time measurement is also possible, although note that some recorded timings may be overestimates when the program is run online, and extremely short presentation rates are not advisable (see Chapter 8 for more details).

If you are wondering whether Flash is right for your research, here are some suggestions for the types of content that can be programmed in Flash: memory experiments, perceptual tasks, simulated games, and any kind of survey to collect information and/or opinions. To help you decide whether to invest time in learning Flash, we've uploaded a sample memory experiment program to http://www.sagepub.com/weinstein to give you an idea of the kind of program you will learn to create. If you work through this book, you will have all the tools at your disposal to create a program like this for your own research.

The following infographic illustrates why Flash is currently the best option for programming online experiments and surveys that will be presented on multiple platforms, as compared with its closest competitor, HTML5. For more information on the software and various purchasing options, please visit http://www.sagepub.com/weinstein.

Comparison of Flash and HTML5.

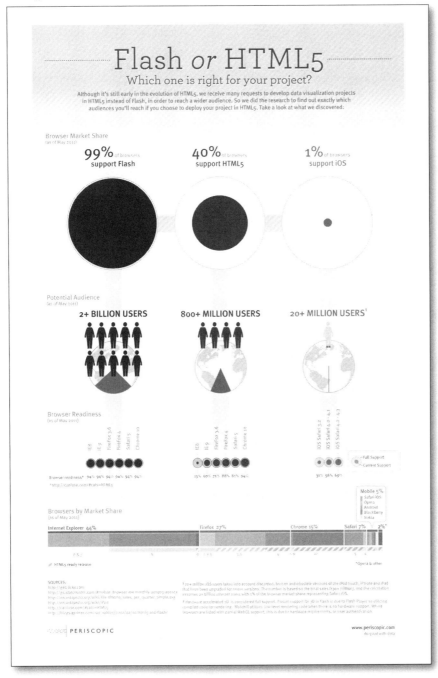

Source: Image Copyright Periscopic, Inc., 2011. http://www.periscopic.com.

Note: This information is correct as of June 2011.

HOW TO USE THIS BOOK

This book has two main uses: It can be used either as a basis for teaching a class, or it can be used as a comprehensive self-study guide. This book neither requires nor assumes any previous knowledge of programming whatsoever, although general computer literacy is necessary. Each chapter introduces a new set of concepts and techniques that are crucial to programming a survey or experiment in Flash. We would go so far as to say that no survey or experiment can be programmed in Flash without some grasp of concepts from each of the chapters. With this in mind, we have designed each chapter to be a hands-on experience to encourage readers to learn and practice all the concepts. Every chapter includes `how-to instructions` and/or `code samples` that can be implemented by typing the code out in a program; each student should do this in order to get a feel for code structure. The code samples are reproduced as they will appear in the Flash interface. In some cases, especially later on, a little setup is needed before the code can be implemented. In these cases, the steps required for setup are listed at the start of the example. All the steps in those setup instructions should already be familiar to the reader as they will have been covered in detail in previous chapters. Most chapters also include an exercise for users to try out on their own. Solutions to these exercises, along with programs associated with each example in the book, are available on the accompanying website.

 ## 1. Teaching a Class Based on the Book

The book itself is based very closely on a semester-long course I taught to psychology graduate students who wanted to learn how to program an experiment for online data collection. Each of the chapters in this book more or less corresponds to one class I taught during the course. Classes were around 3 hours long, and it was a very hands-on course. Each student sat in front of a computer, and I presented short chunks of code on a projector so that students had to type it in to their own program and make it work. If you have a programming background but aren't familiar with Flash, as long as you take a pass through this book on your own first (discussed later), you could run a beginners' programming course on the basis of this book. Simply help the students through each of the examples in a chapter during the class, and set the exercise at the end of the chapter as homework. I found that a ratio of one instructor per four to six students was about right, because students will require a lot of assistance during the learning process. It is amazing how many little things can go wrong in a very simple program! Once students are comfortable with the basics covered in the book, I would set them a larger and more applied task: Program an experiment or survey that they could actually use for their own data collection purposes. This gets students thinking about the design flow of their program and what techniques they really need to master to make their program behave correctly.

2. Using the Book for Self-Study

You can also use this book to teach yourself how to program behavioral experiments and surveys on your own. If this is what you would like to do, we encourage you to use this book as a manual or textbook and not a reference. Studies in cognitive and educational psychology have shown that some of the best learning happens when people take the time to work through problems and experience examples. As such, our recommendation is that you open up a new Flash project and go through this book chapter by chapter, following the instructions laid out for you in each section. Also, if you are new to computer programming, do not expect to learn Flash in one day. The knowledge will stick better if you make the effort to learn ActionScript over a period of several weeks, for instance. If you have the time to set aside, a weekly session of 2 to 3 hours plus some extra time to work on the exercises at the end of each chapter would allow you to cover all the content in the book in 10 weeks.

A special note to Mac users: Most of this book was written based on the Microsoft Windows operating system. As such, you may find several places in this book that do not correspond entirely to what you might be seeing on the screen. However, Flash was developed with both Windows and Macintosh operating systems in mind and you should find these discrepancies to be minimal, if you find them at all. Beginning Mac users should consult their computer manual if they are confused by any instructions within this text. To foreshadow potential issues, windows in OSX can be closed or minimized by clicking the red "X" or yellow "-", respectively, on the top left corner of the window (or press Command-W or Command-M). If your mouse does not support right-clicking, click your mouse while pressing the Control button on your keyboard to mimic a right-click. Certain Mac peripherals may also support right-clicking even if the device doesn't seem to. Again, consult your manual when these issues arise.

 ## 3. Resources

Once you have mastered the basics detailed in the book, you will probably want to move on to more complicated programming. There are many tips, tricks, and advanced techniques that we could not fit into this book, so with this in mind we have compiled a list of resources for each chapter. The links in these resource sections take you to reference tools, tutorials, and pertinent forum discussions that can broaden your horizons and help you become an expert programmer. These links either add extra breadth to a topic covered in the chapter, or they explore a topic that is beyond the scope of this book but could be useful for programming a survey or experiment. The links are mostly to specific articles and tutorials within blogs and websites that post a lot of relevant content, so feel free to explore other content on those blogs and websites, as they may prove to be useful. Each chapter has its own resources section, and there is a web index in the back where the links are listed in alphabetical order. The links are hot-linked for your convenience at http://www.sagepub.com/weinstein.

CHAPTER 1

THE FLASH INTERFACE

IN THIS CHAPTER, YOU WILL LEARN

- How to choose the right type of file for your project
- How to create and save your own ideal workspace
- What all the different tools on your workspace are for
- How to add images and buttons to your project
- That each component in your project needs to have its own unique Instance Name

In this chapter, you will become acquainted with the basics of the Flash interface. Flash is a very versatile and powerful program, so a huge number of tools are available, but we will focus only on those that are essential for programming an experiment or survey. This chapter takes you step by step through choosing the right file type, creating and saving a workspace tailored to your needs, learning about the various panels in this workspace, and adding elements such as buttons and images to your program.

1. Creating a New File

When you open Flash, you have various options for different files you can create (see Figure 1.1 for a screenshot of the menu that pops up when you open Flash).

Figure 1.1. Options for creating a new file in Flash. Adobe product screenshot(s) reprinted with permission from Adobe Systems Incorporated.

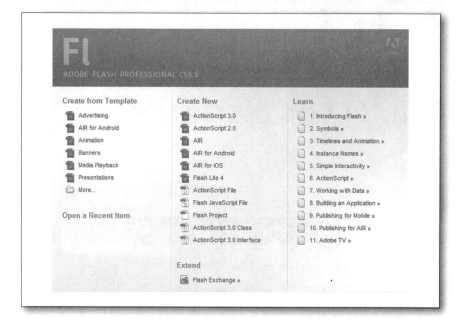

Select the top option in the middle column to create a new ActionScript 3.0 file.

The ActionScript 3.0 file type is the only one we use throughout the book, so you can ignore all the other options. In every chapter we will work on a new Flash program together. To keep things organized and easily match your programs to the sample programs that you can access on the website, save each program with the chapter number in the file name.

2. Managing Your Workspace

As Flash can be used to do all sorts of things (commonly, creating complicated movie clips), there are a lot of tools that Flash provides that you probably won't ever need. In order to set up the most efficient working environment, we will create a workspace that includes only the tools we will use regularly. Various workspaces are already available in Flash, but we will create our own tailored workspace.

To access the different workspaces available within Flash, click on the drop-down menu toward the top right of the screen. This menu should currently say Essentials (see Figure 1.2).

Figure 1.2.   List of available workspaces. Adobe product screenshot(s) reprinted with permission from Adobe Systems Incorporated.

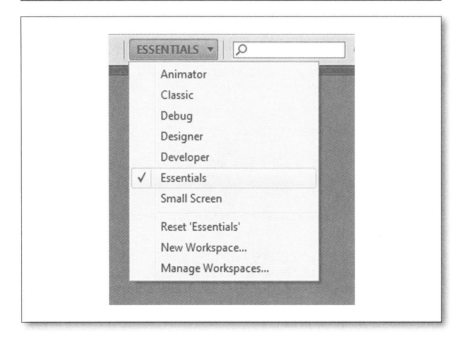

You will see a list of seven workspaces, including Essentials, which is the default. To get an idea of the different workspaces available, try selecting one of the alternatives. We will use a much simpler workspace. Flash allows you to create your own ideal workspace and save it so that you can use it every time.

We will build our workspace from the Small Screen template. You will see a few different panels, some of which we need and some that we will get rid of. The workspace has three docks: the left dock, the right dock, and the bottom dock. You can place any panels in any of these docks. Figure 1.3 is a screenshot of what you should see with the "Small Screen" workspace selected; the three docks have been labeled on the screenshot.

Figure 1.3. "Small Screen" workspace with the three docks labeled. Adobe product screenshot(s) reprinted with permission from Adobe Systems Incorporated.

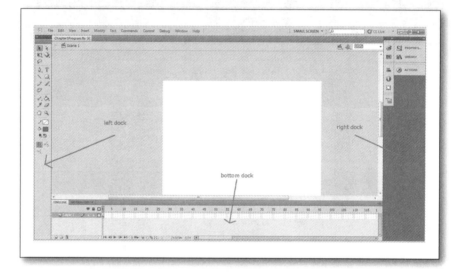

If you do not see any panels after selecting the Small Screen work-space, go to **Windows → Show Panels (F4)**.

Currently in the left dock is the Tools panel. Panels are described in more detail later, but for now just know that you can keep the Tools panel in the left dock as it will come in handy.

Currently in the bottom dock are the Timeline and Motion Editor (click on their tabs to see them). The Timeline can remain where it is, but we do not need the Motion Editor.

To remove the Motion Editor, right-click on its tab and select "Close."

We also need to add two more panels to the bottom dock: Output and Compiler Errors. When you add these panels, they should appear automatically as new tabs in your bottom dock.

> To add Output and Compiler Errors to your bottom dock, go to *Windows* and select each one in turn.

Currently in the right dock, you will find icons for Properties, the Library, and a shortcut to Actions. Those can also remain. In addition, there are a few more toolbars that we should remove, as they are unnecessary.

> To remove the toolbars, drag them away from the dock by clicking on the dotted lines at the top of the toolbar and releasing the icon once it is out of the dock (see Figure 1.4). Then click on the X in the top right corner of the icon to remove it. Repeat for all the groups of icons in the right dock other than Properties, Library, and Actions.

Figure 1.4.   Dragging and removing an icon. Adobe product screenshots for Figures 1.4 and 1.5 reprinted with permission from Adobe Systems Incorporated.

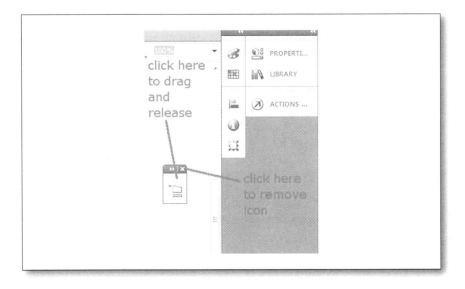

Figure 1.5.   Docking a panel.

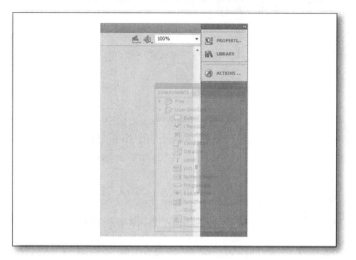

Finally, we need to add the Components and Component Inspector icons to the right dock.

To add the Components icon, go to *Windows → Components (Ctrl+F7)*. To add the Component Inspector icon, go to *Windows → Component Inspector (Shift+F7)*. These panels will appear in the middle of your workspace when you make them visible. To minimize a panel to an icon and dock it in the right dock, drag the panel up underneath the lowermost icon in the dock until its border turns blue (see Figure 1.5). If you release the mouse at this point, the panel will turn into an icon in the dock.

Note that because of the default size of your right dock, you may not be able to see the whole label on each of the icons in the dock. Resize the dock by dragging its left border toward the center. Now that we have our ideal workspace, we need to save it.

To save your workspace, click on the drop-down workspace menu, and select *New Workspace*. Name your workspace "My Workspace."

Now, every time you load Flash, make sure you select "My Workspace" from the drop-down menu. Note that if you change anything on the workspace during a session, the workspace will automatically save these changes.

If you make any unwanted changes, you can choose **Reset 'My Workspace'** from the drop-down menu to revert to the workspace you had at the start of the session.

3. Getting to Know Your Workspace

In this section, we cover all the tools and panels on your workspace. Figure 1.6 is a screenshot of what your workspace should look like after the modifications described earlier, with each of the items labeled to match the descriptions below.

Figure 1.6. An ideal workspace for programming surveys and experiments. Each numbered area is described as follows. Adobe product screenshot(s) reprinted with permission from Adobe Systems Incorporated.

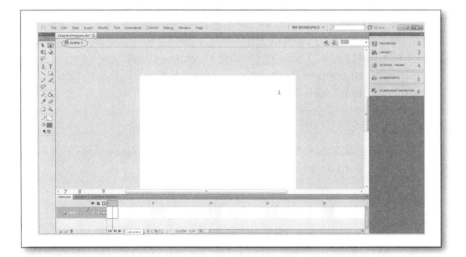

1) Center of Screen: The Stage.

This is the large white square in the middle of your screen. Think of this square as a blank canvas. This is where you place components such as text, pictures, buttons, and so forth; what is on this screen represents what people see when they run the program.

2) Right Dock: Properties Panel.

You use the Properties panel to change the attributes of any objects you use, such as text fields, pictures, buttons, and so forth. Mainly you use this panel to name your components (this will become important when you want to reference them in the code) and change their size. In order to view and edit the properties of any object, select it and click the Properties icon. You can also change the properties of your whole Flash document by clicking on the Properties icon with no object selected. You might want to play with the size of the Stage, as the default size is small. A width by height size of 800 × 600 is a good one as it should fit most browsers, but you could even try 1024 × 768. You could also change the default color of the Stage.

To change the size of the Stage, click on the Properties icon with nothing selected. Under the Properties subheading, change the size to 800 × 600 pixels.

3) Right Dock: The Library.

When you use a component such as a radio button (see "Chapter 6: Questionnaire Tools"), or import an image into the program, these will appear in your Library. There is nothing there right now. You can also use libraries from other open Flash projects, which is why there is a drop-down menu for selecting which file's library you are using.

4) Right Dock: Actions—Frame.

The Actions icon is a shortcut to the window in which you will write your code. You will learn all about that in the next chapter.

5) Right Dock: Components.

Components form the basic building blocks of your program, and they include buttons, check boxes, and lists. Although these various components are described in detail in Chapter 6 on Questionnaire Tools, we use the Button component right away in this chapter.

6) Right Dock: Component Inspector.

The Component Inspector is like a special properties panel specifically for components. Each component has its own set of properties that can be changed in the Component Inspector, and you will learn about these in Chapter 6 (Questionnaire Tools). Note that this panel is only required for

Adobe Flash 5 or earlier. In Flash 5.5, the properties for components are set with the Properties panel.

7)   Bottom Dock: Timeline.

At the moment, the Timeline consists of small rectangles, each of which is a Frame. However, we want to make these bigger so that we can actually see what is on them.

> To enlarge the Frame icons in the Timeline, go to the drop-down menu in the top right corner of the Timeline tab and select *Preview.*

Note that unfortunately, this modification will not save to your workspace, so you will have to do this every time you load Flash.

The Timeline allows you to navigate to any Frame in your project. Frames are typically used in movie clips, but for our purposes, just think of each separate Frame as a different screen in your survey or experiment. For instance, instructions would appear on one Frame, and then the study phase would appear on another. The Frames do not actually have to appear in order on the Timeline, as we are not going to be playing through the Frames like a movie clip. Instead, there will be code associated with each Frame telling the program which Frame to go to next. For more information on Frames, see Chapter 3.

Have a close look at the Timeline. At the moment, only one of the squares that represents the Frames in your project is surrounded by a black border. This means that the other Frames are not there—the blank squares without borders are just placeholders that can have Frames inserted into them. The red rectangle above the first Frame is the playhead, which indicates the Frame that you are on (and hence, the one displayed on the Stage). You will learn how to add new Frames in the next chapter.

On the left-hand side of the Timeline, you will notice the words "Layer 1." Layers are useful for complicated visual layouts, but for our purposes, one layer in the main program will suffice. You can also ignore the tools next to the Layer name, which allow you to lock layers/make them invisible. If you notice that your Timeline has more than one Layer, you may have accidentally double-clicked a component on your Stage and gone into Edit mode. To return to the normal mode, click on "Scene 1" at the top left of your Stage (circled in Figure 1.6).

8) Bottom Dock: Output.

The Output window is where the program displays any information you tell it to output in the code. For instance, you can tell it to display the contents of any variable. We will learn how to do this in the next chapter.

9) Bottom Dock: Compiler Errors.

If there are any problems with your code when you compile it, they appear here with Frame number and line reference, as well as an error code so that you can look up your error. This is what we use for simple debugging. For instance, if you misspell a variable name, or put in an extra character somewhere in the program, it is flagged here. There is also a more advanced Debugger, but it is beyond the scope of this book. Compiler errors are usually enough to help you figure out what is wrong in a relatively simple program.

10) Left Dock: Tools Panel.

If you have used any Adobe products, you will recognize some of these tools. For now, we use two of the tools: the **Selection Tool** (black arrow) and the **Text Tool** (the T).

 ## 4. Adding Elements to Your Stage

You will now learn how to insert images and buttons into your program. This will set you up for learning how to make things happen when buttons are pressed, in the next chapter.

Inserting images is almost as simple as pasting an image into a PowerPoint slide. There is just one extra step—saving the image in the Library for your project.

> To insert an image into your program, paste it onto the Stage. Now click on the Library icon; you will find your image there, named "Bitmap 1." Change its name to something more specific.

If you ever need to use this image again, you can just drag it onto the Stage from your Library. You can now resize the image by clicking on Properties with the image selected. Note that any changes you make to the dimensions of the image when it sits on your Stage will not transfer to the version in the Library.

You can also change the location of the image by editing the X and Y coordinates in the Properties panel, although obviously it is easier to just drag the image by clicking on the selection tool. However, coordinates can be useful for lining things up on different Frames or if you want to change the position of the image from within the code while the program is running.

Inserting a button is also a simple process. A standard button template is available in the Components panel.

> To insert a standard button into your program, first open the Components panel by clicking on the icon. Then look under the *User Interface* folder, where you will find the Button component at the top of the list. Drag this onto the Stage.

Dragging the Button component onto the Stage creates what is called an "instance" of this component. You can think of the actual component as a template. The first thing you need to do with this new instance of the Button component is give it an Instance Name. An Instance Name is a unique name that does not belong to any other object on your Stage and is used to reference the button from the code in order to manipulate it (e.g., make it appear/disappear) or change its appearance. This is crucial for the code you write in Chapter 3 to make something happen when the button is clicked. To make it easier to remember the names of your objects and identify them in the code, try to use Instance Names that are informative and always start with the same abbreviation for each different component. In this book, the prefix "btn" is used for all button Instance Names.

> To give your button an Instance Name, click on Properties with the button selected. Replace <Instance Name> in the top field with "btnEnter."

The instance of the Button component now on your Stage can be resized and given its own label that will be visible to the user (by clicking on Properties with the button selected), but these changes will not affect the Button component.

If you do not like the look of the standard button, there are other options available to you. Figure 1.7 shows a small selection of the available options.

Figure 1.7.   Standard button (top) and a selection of other button templates available in the Library. Adobe product screenshot(s) reprinted with permission from Adobe Systems Incorporated.

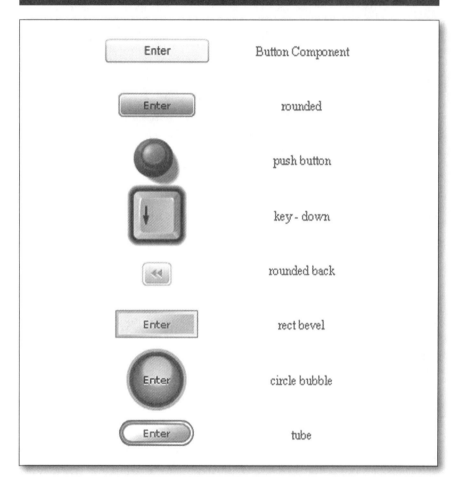

For a larger variety of buttons, go to *Windows → Common Libraries → Buttons*. You will see a drop-down menu of button categories. Click on a category to see what buttons are available. Note that some of the items in the list are not buttons but elements that make up the buttons. To preview a button, click on its name and you will see it appear above the list. Drag a button over to your Stage to add it to your program.

Here you find a large number of arguably visually appealing buttons that can be dragged onto your Stage. They are then copied to your Library so that they can be located easily when you need them again. Remember to give each button on your Stage an Instance Name, and don't forget that no two components on the same Frame can have the same Instance Name.

The only caveat is that editing the label on these buttons is more difficult than with the standard component. To edit the button's label, you need to edit the visual properties of your button, but this is beyond the scope of this book.

Finally, you can also make any image into a button. Please consult the tutorials in the Resources section for how to change the visual properties of buttons and how to create buttons from an image on your Stage.

In this chapter, you learned that we will only use one type of file (the ActionScript 3.0 file type). You also learned that Flash allows you to create and save your own ideal workspace, and you were provided with suggestions for what to include in this workspace. The chapter gave an overview of the various tools you will use most often in your projects. Finally, you took your first step in designing a Flash project by inserting images and buttons to a blank project. Importantly, you learned that every component in your project is given its own unique Instance Name that you can use later to refer to that component in the code. You are now ready to start learning the code that will make your project come to life.

Resources

The following links are hot-linked for your convenience at http://www.sagepub.com/weinstein.

http://tv.adobe.com/channel/how-to/
    Adobe TV, which contains a series of useful how–to videos.

http://www.adobe.com/devnet/flash/articles/flash_cs5_createfla.html
    Another introduction to the Flash workspace.

http://www.video2brain.com/en/videos-699.htm
    A video introducing the Flash interface.

http://www.flashvalley.com/fv_articles/Naming_conventions_in_actionscript/
Some thoughts about naming conventions in Flash.

http://www.webwasp.co.uk/tutorials/005/MX02/index.php
A tutorial about Buttons.

http://www.utexas.edu/learn/flash/buttons.html
Another tutorial about Buttons.

http://www.macloo.com/examples/flash/button_states/
An illustration of the various Button states.

http://www.toxiclab.org/tutorial.asp?ID=69
A tutorial for creating complex Buttons.

CHAPTER 2

ACTIONSCRIPT BASICS

IN THIS CHAPTER, YOU WILL LEARN

- How to use the Actions panel to enter code
- Some very basic Flash terminology and four important coding conventions
- The order in which Flash executes code
- The differences between variable types and how to define a new variable
- How to perform mathematical operations on a Number variable
- How to compile your program and look out for compiler errors
- How to send information to the Output tab
- How to define and call functions and conditional statements
- How to use three different loops to perform repeated actions

In this chapter, we will cover some of the basic terminology, code syntax, and conventions that are all necessary for programming even the most basic experiments. Some of this information might seem a bit abstract right now, but it really does pay to understand these basic concepts from the start. You should work through this chapter first to get the hang of the basics and then use it as a reference when you advance to further chapters, which build upon the concepts introduced here. All you need in order to follow along with this chapter is a new blank ActionScript 3.0 file.

1. Entering Code: Actions Panel

The first thing you need to know to start playing with ActionScript code is where to type it in. The Flash interface does not make this very intuitive.

> To get to the Actions window where you enter code, select a Frame in the Timeline and click on the Actions shortcut button in your right dock. Alternatively, right-click on a Frame in the Timeline and click on *Actions* (at the bottom of the list).

The Actions panel (see Figure 2.1) is divided into three subpanels: the main subpanel on the right where you enter the code, a subpanel that lists all the possible methods you can use in your code, and a subpanel listing all the Frames that have any code attached to them. Every bit of code you write is attached to a particular Frame. To the bottom left of the main subpanel, you will see a tab that indicates which Frame you are currently writing code for and on which Layer the code is being saved (e.g., "Layer 1 : 1" means that you are writing code on Layer 1 for Frame 1). Line numbers appear in the blue column on the left to help you keep track of the code.

Figure 2.1. Actions panel with key features. Adobe product screenshot(s) reprinted with permission from Adobe Systems Incorporated.

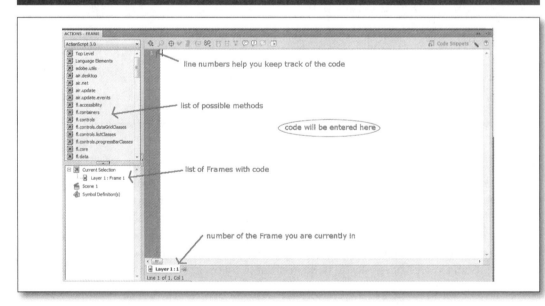

2. Terminology

Knowledge of Flash programming terminology is fundamental because it allows you to communicate accurately and concisely with fellow programmers. Being familiar with commonly used terms in Flash will help immensely if you ever find yourself stuck and need to look either within or outside of this guide for a solution. Here we have compiled the most crucial terms for describing your code:

`Functions` package up a set of instructions for the program to carry out. You give those packages unique names. Then you can call the functions whenever you need them, instead of writing out the same code over and over again in the program.

`Methods` are like functions that have already been defined by ActionScript (instead of by you). Different components have different methods associated with them, which you can look up in the ActionScript Language Reference.

`Properties` can be thought of as adjectives that describe your components. Properties are accessed or changed by writing code that references the property by name (e.g., size).

`Variables` are containers that can store a piece of information. There are different types of variables, which differ according to what sort of information they can store (discussed later).

3. Coding Conventions

It is important to know some basic coding practices at the outset so that you get into good programming habits. Here are some simple tips and conventions to keep in mind:

1) Insert comments throughout your code to explain what each set of actions is for.

These explanatory comments are indispensable for sharing the program with others and helping you understand what a certain piece of code does when you go back to it long after you wrote it. Comments appear grayed out and the program skips over them when executing the code.

To insert a comment into the code, start the line with "//". You will notice that the font immediately turns gray, indicating that this line is ignored by the program. The next line will once again appear in black font and will be read by the program.

```
//This is a comment that explains the code.
```

For longer comments, start the line with "/*". You can then continue the comment on the next line and end it with "*/" whenever you wish. This is also a useful way to disable chunks of code if you are trying to test your program and do not want it to execute some of the code. Remember, everything on a line after "//" or on any lines between "/*" and "*/" is not executed by the program.

```
/*This is a comment

that extends over multiple lines.*/
```

2)   Start every Frame's code with a statement that tells the program to stop on that particular Frame:

```
stop();
```

Unless you do this, if you have multiple Frames in your program Flash will cycle endlessly through the Frames as if they were part of a film strip. If you try typing "stop" into your code, you will notice that the word changes color. This happens to all words that are part of ActionScript 3.0 and are already associated with a component or method in Flash (note that there are various colors that words can take, but the distinction is not important). It would thus be unwise to use any such words to name any of your own variables or functions (more on functions in a minute); if you do, Flash will get confused and think you are asking it to execute the actions associated with that word. When writing code, pay attention to which words change color. If a word that should be a known Flash method does not change color, you may have spelled it wrong; if a word you chose as a name for your variable or function changes color, you should pick a different name.

The empty parentheses after `stop` are where you would put parameters associated with the method—more on that later. The `stop` method does not need to have any parameters associated with it in order for it to work (i.e., no other information is necessary for the statement to execute), so the parentheses remain empty whenever you use this method.

3)   Always end each statement with a semicolon, as in the previous example.

For now, you may be confused about what constitutes a statement and what does not, but this will soon become clear. Although semicolons will not change the way your program is executed, it is a good programming convention to include them because it clearly circumscribes each statement. Using semicolons could also be a lifesaver if your code ever loses its line breaks (e.g., if you copy and paste it into a text file).

4)   Always use the correct capitalization in your methods and when calling variables and functions.

ActionScript is case-sensitive: "Stop" with a capital "S" will not do the same thing as "stop" with a lowercase "s" (in fact, it won't do anything). If you have typed what you believe to be a known ActionScript method and it does not change color, check your capitalizations. Misspellings are also the most common cause of errors when the program tries to compile. If you have misspelled a variable or function name, the program will think you are referring to an object that does not exist.

A convention used in this book and in most online code samples is related to capitalization—names of functions, methods, properties, and variables all begin with a lowercase letter. If the name includes more than one word or abbreviation, the first letter of the second word is usually capitalized (and do note that spaces cannot be used). Thus, you should try to write names such as "score," "subjectScore," and "subjectScoreA," but never names like "Score," "subjectscore," or "subject score."

4. Order of Execution

When you enter a Frame, Flash reads the code from left to right, top to bottom. All code that is not contained within a function will execute immediately in the order that it is written. Functions themselves will not execute unless they are explicitly called from within the code or when an event that triggers the function occurs. Events can include user input such as mouse clicks or key presses and those that occur within the program such as a timer expiring.

The order of execution also applies to code within a function. A mistake in the order of written statements within the code is often responsible for unexpected behavior from your program. For instance, imagine you have a function that saves user input from a text field and clears the text field so that the user can answer the next question. If you write the statement that clears the text field before the statement that saves the user input, you will be unable to save the input because the field has already been cleared.

 ## 5. Variables

Table 2.1 summarizes the main variable types that we use throughout this book.

Table 2.1.	Data types and examples.	
Data type	Example	Description
Number	4.5	Any number, including floating point values (decimals)
int	−5	Any integer or whole number
String	"hello"	Text or a string of characters
Boolean	true	True or False
Array	[2, 9, 17]	More than one value in a single variable

When you define a new variable, you need to give it a name that is unique to the variable. You will then use that name to reference the variable later on.

```
    /*This  is  how  you  define  three  different
variables*/
    var myNumber:Number = new Number;

    var myInteger:int = new int;

    var myString:String = new String;

    /*After you have defined them, assign values to
your variables like this:*/
    myNumber = 2.345;

    myInteger = 10;

    myString = "I am learning Flash!";
```

You can also assign a value to the variable in the same line as you define it (note that you can only use this code OR the code which separates the definition and value assignment into two lines; if you use both, Flash will throw up an error because you are defining the same variable twice in one project):

```
var myNumber:Number = 2.345;

var myInteger:int = 10;

var myString:String = "I am learning Flash!";
```

The "=" sign used here is not an "equals" sign as you might intuit—instead, it is commonly called "gets" (i.e., "myNumber gets 2.345"). What this means is that, in this example, the variable name myNumber now refers to the value that has been assigned to it; in a sense, myNumber becomes 2.345. In subsequent code, you can now use myNumber whenever you want to use the value stored in this variable. (You will learn later on that to check for equality, you will use the double equals operator, or "==.")

6. Simple Mathematical Operations

The easiest way to become acquainted with ActionScript is to get the program to do some simple math. We start by creating a Number variable and then we manipulate this variable with some basic operations. To follow along with this example, delete the code you entered in the previous example or start with a new blank ActionScript 3.0 file, but remember to put `stop();` at the top of the Frame.

```
/*Create a Number variable and give it an
initial value of 0*/

var myNumber:Number = 0;
```

Performing mathematical operations in Flash is easy. Just remember that a mathematical statement with an equals sign will assign the value on the right of the equation to the variable identified on the left of the equation. See the Resources for a link to a list of acceptable mathematical operations.

```
/*Here are a few mathematical operations to try*/

myNumber = myNumber + 5;

myNumber = myNumber - 10;

myNumber = myNumber * 3;

myNumber = myNumber / 2;
```

7. Compiling the Program

You are now ready to compile the program. At the moment, nothing interesting is going to happen when the program is compiled, but you can check to see if you have any errors in your code.

To compile the program, press *Ctrl+ENTER* in Windows or ⌘+*ENTER* on a Mac.

You should now see a pop-up screen with the contents of your Stage; for now it is blank. Compiling the program creates a .swf file in the same folder as your .fla file. This is a movie version of your program, which you can run but not edit.

If you have made any errors in your code (e.g., a misspelled variable name), they will appear in the Compiler Errors tab. The error message will include a reference to the Frame and line in which the error occurs. For instance, if you misspell the name of a variable, Flash will not recognize what you are asking it to do. Imagine you type the following code:

```
var myNumber:Number = new Number;

mynumber = 1;
```

Because Flash is case sensitive, the variable "mynumber" will not be recognized, and you will get the error message shown in Figure 2.2.

Figure 2.2. Compiler error resulting from misspelling the variable name "myNumber" as "mynumber." Adobe product screenshot(s) reprinted with permission from Adobe Systems Incorporated.

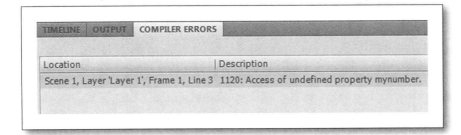

TIMELINE	OUTPUT	COMPILER ERRORS	

Location	Description
Scene 1, Layer 'Layer 1', Frame 1, Line 3	1120: Access of undefined property mynumber.

For a list of the most common errors people make in their programs, see the link in the Resources section. If you receive an error that is not listed there, try googling the phrase to see what other programmers have done to eliminate the error.

8. Sending Information to the Output Tab

It would now be useful to actually see the result of your mathematical operations. Right now, if you compile the program, the operations will be carried out, but you will not be shown the result. To get the program to produce visible information, we use the `trace` method, which sends information to the Output tab for you to view while the program is running. In order to see the contents of a variable at any given time, simply type "trace" followed by the variable name in parentheses.

```
    /*Add this line of code whenever you want to
trace the contents of your Number variable.*/

    trace(myNumber);
```

Note that you need to include this line of code after every mathematical operation in the previous example if you want to output the result of each calculation. To make the most use out of the `trace` method, you can also include any text you like with the output, kind of like a comment. Enclose the text in quotation marks, and notice that it goes green. In this book, quoted text is shown in light blue, but in your code it should be green.

```
myNumber = myNumber/2;

    trace("the result of dividing my number by 2 is",
myNumber);
```

 ## 9. Functions

Functions are just packages of instructions for the program to carry out. Functions are named in the same way variables are—you simply give your new function a unique name, and use that name to call the function later.

```
    /*Here's how you define a function (but do not
type this into your program yet, as the bolded
words are just placeholders)*/

    function functionName(<input>):<output>

    {

        //This is where your actions will go;

    }
```

The <input> and <output> placeholders are parameters of the function, and the grayed out comment is where the events that take place when the function is executed will go. The input parameter is used when the function is called by an action from the user. For instance, if you are going to get the function to execute when the user clicks a mouse button (see Chapter 3) or presses a key (see Chapter 4), you need to include that information in the input. The output parameter is used to pass information out of the function. We do not need to worry about that until a later chapter ("Chapter 5: Presenting and Storing Information in Arrays"). If you are going to be calling the function from the code instead of in response to a user's actions, you do not need an input or an output. In this case, you would leave the parentheses empty and put "void" where there would be output:

```
/*This function will perform a mathematical
operation*/

function functionName():void

{

    myNumber = myNumber/2;

    trace("The function was executed and myNumber
is equal to", myNumber);

}
```

If you enclose the mathematical operations you were trying out earlier in the chapter within a function, you will notice that the operation does not occur if you compile your program. This is because the function needs to be called first. Calling a function from the code is very easy. You simply type the name of the function with empty parentheses to indicate that you are not passing any input to the function:

```
functionName();
```

Whenever you type the name of your function like this in the code, it will immediately execute. Another way to execute a function is in response to an event, such as the user pressing a button. This is covered in the next chapter.

10. Conditional Statements

Understanding conditional statements is also a prerequisite for Flash programming. These logical arguments allow you to make different things happen depending on whether certain conditions are met. For instance, you might have different versions of the program with different sets of questions, or the user's response to one question may determine whether the user is asked another. With a conditional statement, you tell the program to check whether a certain condition is met. If this condition is met, a set of actions is executed. This is the basis of a simple if/then statement.

```
    /*Syntax for a basic if/then statement (bolded
phrase will be replaced with a statement)*/

    if (<first condition to be satisfied>)

    {

    //This is where your actions will go;

    }
```

Note that even though the statement implies "if . . . then . . .," you do not have to type the word "then." Instead, the action to be carried out is contained within curly brackets after the word if or else if or else.

To describe the condition that needs to be satisfied in order for an action to be performed, use two equals signs "==" to mean "is" (see one of the links in the Resources section for other useful conditional operators). Be careful not to use a single equals sign, which will simply change your variable to be equal to that value (as in the previous mathematical operations).

You can add the following code to the program you have been working on, where you perform various mathematical operations on the variable "myNumber."

```
    /*This code checks the result of your math
operation and traces a message if the result is
10*/

    if (myNumber == 10)

    {

        trace("Perfect Ten!");

    }
```

Try out this code with various values and mathematical operations on myNumber; you should get the "Perfect Ten!" message traced in the Output when the result of the mathematical operation is 10. If this is not happening, make sure that the conditional statement checking the result of your operation comes after the operation in the code.

You can build on your `if` statement by adding additional conditions using `else if`.

```
if (myNumber == 10)

{

    trace ("Perfect Ten!");

}
else if (myNumber < 10)

{

    trace ("under ten");

}
else if (myNumber > 10)

{

    trace ("over 10");

}
```

Initially, the program will determine whether the first condition is satisfied (in this example, whether "myNumber" is equal to 10). If the first condition is satisfied, the actions in the first curly brackets will be carried out and the remaining code in the `else if` statements will be skipped. If the first condition is not satisfied (here, if myNumber is not equal to 10), the program moves on to the second condition—the one listed under `else if`—and repeats the same process. You can have as many `else if` statements as you like, and the program will work through them sequentially from top to bottom until a condition is satisfied.

You can also include a catch-all `else` condition. If no conditions are satisfied, the actions under `else` will be performed.

```
if (myNumber == 10)

{
```

Box (Continued)

```
Box (Continued)
        trace("Perfect Ten!");

    }

    else

    {

        trace("Try again!");

    }
```

Note that you are not obliged to include the else statement. If you have no else statement, the program will not carry out any actions unless one of the conditions is satisfied.

When writing conditional statements, do not get confused between a string of if statements and a statement with multiple conditions. For instance, consider the following two sets of statements:

```
    /*This set of conditional statements will
output "Perfect Ten!" if myNumber is equal to 10,
and "Not Bad!" if myNumber is not equal to 10 but
is larger than 5.*/
    if(myNumber == 10)

    {

        trace("Perfect Ten!")

    }
    else if(myNumber > 5)

    {

        trace("Not Bad!")


    }

    /*This set of conditional statements, on the
other hand, will output "Perfect Ten!" if myNumber
```

```
is equal to 10, and it will also output "Not Bad!"
if myNumber is larger than 5 (even if it is equal
to 10).*/

    if(myNumber == 10)

    {

        trace("Perfect Ten!")

    }

    if(myNumber > 5)

    {

        trace("Not Bad!")

    }
```

Here is another worked out example that demonstrates the use of conditionals in more depth. Say that you are a professor who wants to write a program to determine if a student needs extra tutoring. You assess that student's knowledge (on a 0-100 scale) on four domains named domain1, domain2, domain3, and domain4. You decide that a student needs tutoring if any of those domains receive a failing grade (less than a 60, for our purposes) or if the overall average score of those domains is less than a 75. Here is how you would use conditionals to make this judgment:

```
    if(domain1 < 60 || domain2 < 60 || domain3 < 60
|| domain4 < 60)

    {

        trace("You  need  tutoring  for  failing  a
    domain.");

    }

    else if ((domain1 + domain2 + domain3 + domain4)
/ 4 < 75)

    {
```

Box (Continued)

```
Box (Continued)
      trace("You need tutoring for getting a low
   average.");

   }


   else

   {

      trace("You do not need tutoring!")

   }
```

Note that the first line of code makes use of the "pipes" (i.e., "||"). This symbol represents an inclusive OR. Thus, the if statement is triggered if any of the four substatements are true; namely, if any of the four domains score less than 60. You can also use "&&" to represent AND. If you swapped && out for || every time it appeared on line one, the "You need tutoring for failing a domain" message would only display if EVERY domain scored less than 60.

Here is another example. Say you want to write an algorithm to determine if an individual is eligible to become president of the United States. The U.S. Constitution requires one to meet three requirements to be president: (1) the individual must be a natural-born citizen, (2) he or she must be at least 35 years of age, and (3) this person must have been a permanent resident for at least 14 years.

We happen to have this information saved already—the person's age as an int, his or her citizenship as a Boolean (true—a citizen—or false—not), and his or her time spent as a citizen as another int.

This is easy to do. We could write this:

```
if (age >= 35)

{

   if (citizen == true)

   {
```

```
        if (timeSpent >= 14)
            {
                trace("This person can become
president.");
            }
        }
    }
```

11. Loops

Loops allow you to execute a piece of code repeatedly. You use loops if you want to do the same thing to a set of items, for instance, to every element in an Array (see Chapter 5). The following different types of loops each have their own advantages:

For loops define a counter to keep track of the number of times the code in the loop has executed, and exit the loop when the counter reaches the specified value.

While loops define a condition, and the loop keeps executing until the condition is no longer true.

Do while loops are the same as while loops, but the actions are executed once regardless of whether the condition is true, and then the loop keeps executing until the condition is no longer true.

To follow along with this example, make sure you have defined the myNumber variable in your current project. To make the for loop work, you need to give it four pieces of information:

1) The initial value of the counter

2) The value at which the counter should stop iterating

3) The increment to the counter on each loop

4) What actions to execute on each loop

```
    /*Here is a for loop that multiplies myNumber
by itself each time the loop executes*/

    //This for loop will execute five times;

    var i:int = 0;

    for(i = 0; i < 5; i++)

    {

        myNumber = myNumber * myNumber;

    trace("loop number: ", i, "myNumber = ",
myNumber)

    }
```

Looking at the definition of the for loop (right after the word `for`), the first statement (i = 0) indicates that the initial value of the counter (i) is set at 0. The next statement (i < 5) indicates that the value at which the counter should stop iterating is set at 5. That is, the loop will execute when the counter is at 0, 1, 2, 3, and 4, but not once the counter reaches 5. The third statement (i++) indicates that each time the loop executes, 1 is added to the counter.

Looking now at the actions in the for loop, each time the loop executes, the first line multiples myNumber by itself. The next line outputs the loop number and the result of the mathematical operation.

To make a while loop work, all you need to define is a condition that will stop the loop when it is no longer satisfied (make sure you still have a variable called myNumber defined in your project to try out this code):

```
    /*The following while loop executes the same
actions as the previous for loop, but it stops when
myNumber exceeds 100:*/

    myNumber = 5;

    while (myNumber < 100)

    {
```

```
    myNumber=myNumber * myNumber;

    trace("the while loop executed and myNumber
=" myNumber);

    }
```

This loop continues to execute until "myNumber" is no longer smaller than 100. If this loop does not seem to be executing, check to see if the original value of "myNumber" is larger than 100. Although while loops might seem more straightforward than for loops, the danger with while loops is that you might accidentally write an "infinite" loop, one that never exits because the condition you set is never met. Have a look at the following example (but don't try this code out, or the program will crash—we have put the code in a comment just in case):

```
/*An example of an infinite while loop:

myNumber = 5;

while(myNumber > 1)

{

    myNumber=myNumber * myNumber;

    trace(myNumber);

}*/
```

Because "myNumber" is always going to be greater than 1, this while loop will execute infinitely and the program will not be able to continue on to the next actions.

The do while loop is exactly the same as a while loop except that the actions in the loop will execute once even if the condition for exiting the loop has already been met.

```
//The following do while loop will execute once:

myNumber = 5;
```

Box (Continued)

```
Box (Continued)
    do

    {

        myNumber = myNumber * myNumber;

        trace(myNumber);

    }

    while (myNumber < 5)
```

Exercise: This function is supposed to guess the height (in feet) of a child, depending on his or her age (in years).

```
if (age <= 1)

{

height = 1.5;

}

if (age <= 5)

{

height = 4.5;

}

else

{

height = 5;

}
```

Without typing this code into your program to test it, answer the following question: What height will the conditional statement output for the following ages: 1, 4, and 8 years? Now rewrite the conditional statements so that they produce different estimates for different ages.

In this chapter, you learned that code is entered in the Actions panel and each chunk of code you enter is linked to a specific Frame. You then learned four important definitions: `functions`, `methods`, `properties`, and `variables`. Next, you learned about four important coding conventions: 1) using comments throughout the code as explanations, 2) starting every Frame's code with the statement `stop()`, 3) ending each statement with a semicolon, and 4) using correct capitalization throughout your code. You then discovered the order in which Flash reads your code (everything in the current Frame is read from top to bottom, except for code contained in functions, which is only read when that function is called).

Next you learned about variable types, each of which stores a different type of information. Focusing on one of these variables types (`Number`), you learned how to perform basic mathematical operations. Once your first program was ready, you learned that you can compile it by pressing *Crtl+ENTER* or *⌘+ENTER*. You then discovered two important windows: Compile Errors, where you are informed about any bugs in your program, and Output, where you can send information from your program.

You also learned a lot of coding basics in this chapter: how to define and call functions, how to write conditional statements so that actions are executed only when certain conditions are met, and how to define loops so that actions can be repeated multiple times. This chapter is full of useful basic information that you might forget later on, so do use it as a reference point.

12. Resources

The following links are hot-linked for your convenience at http://www.sagepub.com/weinstein.

http://help.adobe.com/en_US/flash/cs/using/WS3e7c64e37a1d85e1e229
110db38dec34-7feba.html
Discusses the "code hinting" feature in Flash.

http://www.sunilb.com/programming/12-common-programming-mistakes-
to-avoid
Common programming mistakes.

http://www.foundation-flash.com/tutorials/debugging/
Common errors people make in Flash and how to fix them.

http://home.earthlink.net/~craie/121/notes/vocabulary.html
Programming language vocabulary basics.

http://www.adobe.com/livedocs/flash/9.0/main/wwhelp/wwhimpl/common/
html/wwhelp.htm?context=LiveDocs_Parts&file=00000047.html
Flash data type reference.

http://flash-creations.com/notes/actionscript_operators.php
Common mathematical operators in Flash.

http://www.actionscript.org/forums/showthread.php3?t=177515
A forum discussion of what precisely "void" means in functions.

http://www.actionscript.org/resources/articles/5/1/The-power-of-nested-
loops/Page1.html
Using "nested for loops" in Flash.

CHAPTER 3

NAVIGATION

IN THIS CHAPTER, YOU WILL LEARN

- To use a flowchart to plan your program
- How to insert and name new Frames
- How to make Flash respond to an event
- How to write a function that jumps from Frame to Frame
- How to use Frame numbers and names for navigation
- How to reuse a function
- How to remove Event Listeners to maintain clean code

Many programmers will conceptualize their programs in terms of a flowchart: A certain answer to a prompt will determine what happens next. In this chapter, we discuss how to move from one element of the flowchart to another. The experimenter needs to be able to do this in order to direct where the user will go next. That is, clicking a button might let the user proceed from the instructions to the experiment itself, or proceed to the next question, or perhaps to go back to a previous question in order to change an answer. To make this happen, the programmer must write code that tells the program what to show the user at each step in the flowchart.

The following flowchart (see Figure 3.1) may be humorous, but the message is true: Always start with a flowchart. In this chapter, we build a program that takes the user through the steps in this flowchart.

Figure 3.1.   Example of a simple flowchart.

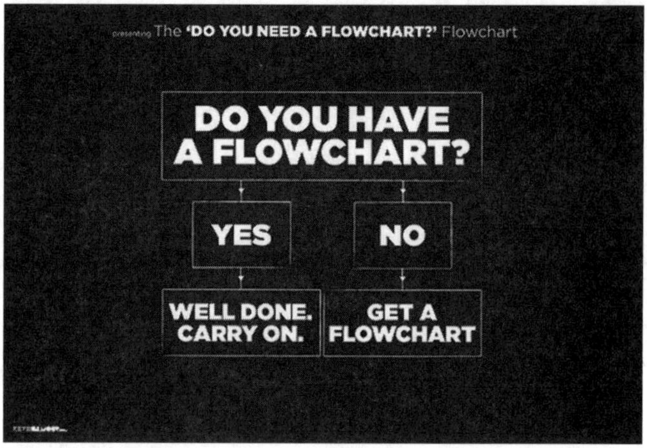

Source: Kevin Gilmour/flickr

1. Inserting New Frames

You will probably use a new Frame each time you significantly change what you are presenting to the user in terms of layout and formatting. For instance, you might have one Frame for instructions, although multiple screens of instructions could be presented by refreshing the text without changing to a new Frame (see Chapter 4). Another example would be a multitrial experiment where you are presenting participants with lists of words. It would be inefficient to use a separate Frame for each word in the list but sensible to change Frames for the recognition test following the study phase, as this would need to have a different layout. In essence, you can think of each Frame as a template.

For the program in this chapter, we treat each of the steps in the flowchart as a separate Frame, so we need three Frames (one for the question and one for each of the two outcomes). If you go to your Timeline in a new project, you will see that there is only one Frame in your project. You have two main options for inserting a new Frame.

> To insert a new blank Frame, right-click on an empty placeholder and select *Insert Blank Keyframe*.

> To insert a new Frame that is a copy of the previous frame, right-click on an empty placeholder and select *Insert Keyframe*.

You will also see the option ***Insert Frame*** in the menu. Do not select this option because it will create a Frame that cannot have any code attached to it. These types of frames are used in animations. Since we are using Flash for a completely different purpose, we want each Frame to accept code, so we always use Keyframes.

2. Naming Frames

There are two main ways you can navigate between Frames. One way is by using the Frame numbers automatically assigned to each Frame you add in the Timeline. The first Frame that is already in the Timeline when you create a new program is numbered Frame 1, and subsequent Frames are numbered consecutively.

Another way is by naming each Frame and referring to that name in the code when you want to jump to it. The Frame numbers method is easier because you do not have to worry about naming Frames. However, if you change the order of the Frames in the Timeline, you will have to change the code to reference the correct Frames. It may also become difficult to remember which Frame contains which step of your program if you use many Frames. We therefore recommend giving each of your Frames a descriptive name and using these names for navigation.

> To name a Frame, click on it in the Timeline and then click on Properties. Name the Frame under *LABEL → Name*.

Be sure to use different names for each of your Frames. The program will still compile if you have named more than one Frame the same thing, but it will issue a warning indicating where you have the duplicate (see Figure 3.2).

Figure 3.2.   Duplicate label warning. Adobe product screenshot(s) reprinted with permission from Adobe Systems Incorporated.

```
TIMELINE   OUTPUT   COMPILER ERRORS
   WARNING: Duplicate label, Scene=Scene 1, Layer=Layer 1, Frame=4, Label=flowchart
```

To follow along with the example in this chapter, you need to create three Frames and name them as follows:

1)   "flowchart"

2)   "wellDone"

3)   "getAFlowchart"

You will learn much more about manipulating text in Chapter 4, but for now just click on the Text tool (the T) and add the following text to each Frame:

1)   "Do you have a flowchart?"

2)   "Well done. Carry on."

3)   "Get a flowchart."

Finally, you need to add two buttons to Frame 1: one that says "Yes" and another that says "No." Give these buttons the Instance Names "btnYes" and "btnNo," respectively. Refer to "Chapter 1: The Flash Interface" for instructions on how to add and name buttons.

 ## 3. Responding to a Button Press

We are going to write code that makes the program jump to a new Frame when the user hits a button. To understand the code, you need to understand the logic ActionScript uses to execute statements.

The code that we need to write in order to respond to a button press consists of two components: one part that tells the program to expect the button press and the other part that tells the program what to do when the button is pressed. The first part is called the event listener, because it tells the program to listen out for an event (in this case, a button press, but event listeners can listen out for many different events such as key strokes or a certain amount of time passing). The second part of the code is a function, which contains instructions for what the program should do when this function is called. The event listener code responds to the button press by calling and executing the function. Following is a template for code that listens for a button press and triggers a function. We will write the function itself later. Do not type this code into your program yet, because we still need to replace the bolded placeholders with the appropriate information.

```
<target>.addEventListener(<EventType.EVENT_
NAME>, <functionName>);
```

Before we can replace the placeholders with specified information, we need to understand the code, so let us examine each part of the code in turn.

`<target>` refers to whatever object you would like the user to be able to interact with. In this case, it is a button. It could also be a text field or the whole Stage itself. The event listener will only listen out for an event that happens to the target referenced here. For instance, if you reference a button, it will only respond to that button and not any other button on the Stage. This placeholder should be replaced with the Instance Name of the relevant component on your Stage (refer to Chapter 1 for instructions on how to place an instance of a button on your Stage and give it a unique Instance Name). In this case, we would need two event listeners, one with the target "btnNo" and the other with the target "btnYes."

`addEventListener` is a known Flash method that tells the program to listen out for an event; you do not need to replace this term.

`<EventType>` determines what sort of event is to be listened out for. There are far too many different types of events (and specific events within these types) to summarize here (see the Resources for a link to the complete list). For now, we want the button to respond to a mouse click, so the type of event we need to reference here is `MouseEvent`.

`<EVENT_NAME>` is the specific event within the specified event type that we want the program to listen out for and respond to. Here, we want the program to listen out for a mouse click on the button, so we replace the placeholder with `CLICK`. Note that the event name is always in all caps. Again, check the Resources for a link to the complete list of events the program can respond to.

`<eventResponse>` is a placeholder for the name of the function that is called when the relevant event occurs. Since the functions in our example are going to execute when No or Yes buttons are pressed, let us call our two functions "functionNo" and "functionYes." Function names can be whatever you want, but try to think of function names that are descriptive so that you can keep track of all the functions in your program.

```
//Adding an EventListener to the button "btnNo";

btnNo.addEventListener(MouseEvent.CLICK,
functionNo);
```

All the words should now be blue other than the name of your button and the name of your function. If they are not, check your spelling and capitalization. Note that the line of the code that adds an event listener is a statement, so it needs to end with a semicolon.

```
//Adding an EventListener to the button "btnYes";

btnYes.addEventListener(MouseEvent.CLICK,
functionYes);
```

 ## 4. Code for Frame Navigation

The previous code is not a stand-alone code. In fact, if you tried to execute this code by compiling the program, you would receive the error messages shown in Figure 3.3.

Figure 3.3. Error due to referencing a function that has not been defined. Adobe product screenshot(s) reprinted with permission from Adobe Systems Incorporated.

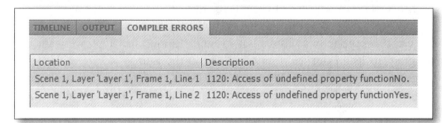

This is because the event listener is triggering a function that you have not yet defined. Remember from Chapter 2 that functions in general are built on the following framework:

```
function <functionName>(<input>):<output>
{
    //Actions to be executed;
}
```

<functionName> should match the name of the function you refer-enced in the event listener. In this case, you will have two functions, one called "functionYes" and the other "functionNo."

<input> will be the event that is triggering the function. In this case, the function is triggered by a mouse click, so the appropriate input is MouseEvent (for a link to lists of possible events, consult the Resources section). It is important to include the right input, otherwise the function will not execute. There is no output associated with this function, so we replace that field with the word void.

As we have already discussed, you should normally put a semicolon after each line of code. However, the line that defines your function and its param-eters is one exception to this rule; you should NOT put a semicolon after the end of this line. If you do, the system will not process the subsequent lines of code correctly. (You can think of an entire function as existing in one line of code, spread out over several to make reading and editing it easier.) Do, however, put a semicolon after each statement within your function.

```
    /*The following code defines the function but
does not yet include the actions that take place
when the function is executed.*/

    function functionYes(evt:MouseEvent):void

    {

        //Actions to be executed;

    }
```

The curly brackets encompass the body of the function. This is where you place any code that you want to be executed when the function is called. Here we use the gotoAndStop() method, which makes the program jump to which-ever Frame we reference in parentheses. The Frame can be referenced either by its number in the Timeline or the name assigned to it in the Properties Inspector.

```
    //You can call a Frame by its number;

    gotoAndStop(2);

    //You can also call a Frame by its name;

    gotoAndStop("wellDone");
```

Note that if you are using a Frame name, this must be encompassed in quotation marks. Otherwise, the program will think you are referencing a variable.

Here is all the code we need to listen out for the button press and proceed to the next Frame when the user clicks the button (if you are trying out this code, make sure that you have inserted and appropriately named Frame 2 in your Timeline; see section 2 of this chapter):

```
stop();

btnYes.addEventListener(MouseEvent.CLICK,
functionYes);

function functionYes(evt:MouseEvent):void

{

    gotoAndStop("wellDone");

}
```

Exercise 1: Now that you know how to write a function that sends the user to a different Frame, try adding the function that responds to the "No" button. When that works, try using Frame numbers instead of Frame names to navigate through your program.

 ## 5. Reusing Functions

One important thing to consider when you are writing code is that you should not have to write a new function every time you want something to happen. In the previous example, we only wanted the user to be able to skip from one Frame to two others, so having separate functions for each of the buttons was OK. However, imagine your program consisted of 10 Frames, and you wanted the user to go from Frame 1 to Frame 2, and then from Frame 2 to Frame 3, and so on. One way to solve this problem is to have a new button with a unique Instance Name, a new event listener on each Frame that will send you to the appropriate next Frame. Instead of this lengthy solution, you could achieve the same behavior by reusing the same button, the same event listener, and the same function.

To follow along with this example, you need to do the following:

1) Start a new project.

2) Add at least five Blank Keyframes to your Timeline (there is no need to name your Frames for this example).

3) Add a button to each Frame.

4) Give all the buttons the Instance Name "btnNavigate." (Hint: If you copy and paste the button onto each subsequent Frame, the Instance Name will copy over too.)

5) Define a new function called "changeFrame," but leave the actions blank for now.

6) Add an event listener that responds to the button "btnNavigate" and calls the function "changeFrame".

Note that the advice to name the buttons on each screen with the same Instance Name may seem counter to what you learned about Instance Names. You are allowed to name the buttons the same thing in this case because they will be on different Frames. The same button is essentially appearing on each Frame.

To create a reusable function for navigating through your program, you need to perform the following steps:

1) Create a variable to store the number of the Frame you want to jump to.

2) Create a function that uses the `gotoAndStop` method to change frames.

3) Reference the variable that holds the number of the Frame you want to jump to in the `gotoAndStop` method.

4) Change the contents of the variable whenever you want to change where the program will jump to on the next button click.

As you will remember from the previous chapter, there are a few different variable types (if you do not remember, please reread the relevant section of the chapter). To navigate by Frame number, we use the `int` (short for integer) variable type, which stores whole numbers (i.e., no decimals or fractions).

```
    /*Define a new int variable to store the Frame
number you want to navigate to next.*/

    var nextFrameNumber = new int;
```

Now you need to write a statement in your function that uses the gotoAndStop method to direct the program to the relevant Frame:

```
    /*The following code should be inside your
"changeFrame" function*/

    gotoAndStop(nextFrameNumber);
```

Note that unlike Frame names, variable names should not be enclosed in quotation marks. If you put the variable name in quotations, Flash will read the variable name as a text string and will look for a Frame called "nextFrame-Number" instead of looking for the relevant variable.

The last step is to define the contents of the "nextFrameNumber" variable on each Frame. Since we want the program to jump from Frame 1 to Frame 2 and then from Frame 2 to Frame 3, the variable should be assigned the integer 2 on Frame 1 and the integer 3 on Frame 2 (i.e., the number of the next Frame we want to jump to).

```
    /*For example, you would put the following code
in Frame 1*/

    nextFrameNumber = 2;
```

To sum up, you now have an event listener and a function defined on Frame 1. You then change the contents of the variable "nextFrameNumber" on each subsequent Frame to determine where the program jumps to when the button is clicked.

```
    var nextFrameNumber:int = new int;

    btnNavigate.addEventListener(MouseEvent.CLICK,
changeFrame);

    nextFrameNumber = 2;
```

```
function changeFrame(evt:MouseEvent):void

{

    gotoAndStop(nextFrameNumber);

}
```

To advance from Frame 2 to Frame 3, all you need to do is put the code `nextFrameNumber = 3` in the Actions for that Frame. Remember that the code in the Frame is read by that program as soon as that Frame is loaded, so the next time you click on the button it will take you to Frame 3.

6. Removing Event Listeners

Just as we can add event listeners, we can also remove them. When and why would we want to do this? There are times when you might want to change what happens when a button is clicked. In that case, you would remove the event listener that triggers one function and add an event listener that triggers another. If you did not remove the first event listener, both functions would be triggered when the button was pressed. Another example of when you might want to remove an event listener is if you want to deactivate a button. To remove an event listener, use the `removeEventListener` method (instead of `addEventListener`). The rest of the code stays exactly the same as when you added the event listener:

```
btnNavigate.removeEventListener(MouseEvent.
CLICK, changeFrame);
```

Another good reason to always remove event listeners when they become redundant is to prevent Flash from overloading its resources. It's also good practice in general to make sure that all the processes taking place while your program is running are currently necessary, and removing event listeners is one way to make sure this is the case.

Exercise 2: Write a function or functions that allow(s) you to navigate forward and backward through three Frames. On Frame 1 you can only go forward, on Frame 2 you can go forward to Frame 3 or back to Frame 1, and on Frame 3 you can only go back to Frame 1. See the flowchart in Figure 3.4.

Figure 3.4.   Flowchart for Frame navigation Exercise 2.

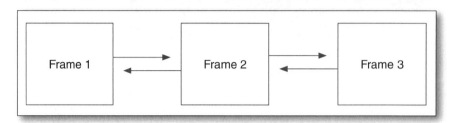

In this chapter, you learned that flowcharts are a very important tool for planning your programs. We used a silly but effective flowchart to build a simple program that takes the user through a series of Frames with different content. To do this, you learned how to insert new Frames and that you can use the Frame number or a unique name to refer to each Frame. You also learned that if you want to make the program respond to an event, you need to write what is called an "event listener." This is somewhat counterintuitive, but it is very important to understand. The event you made Flash respond to in this chapter was a mouse click, but other events will come up in later chapters. You learned not only how to add event listeners but also how to remove them when they are no longer useful, to reduce clutter in your program.

In this chapter, you wrote a function that caused the screen to jump from Frame to Frame and display different content to the user. You used both Frame numbers and names to achieve this content change. Finally, you learned that you do not have to write a new function every time you want something to happen.

The techniques covered in this chapter are directly applicable to presenting users with instructions before and during a survey or experiment. For instance, you might want to show individuals a welcome screen, followed by several screens (Frames) of instructions. You might provide "Forward" and "Back" buttons in case people want to go back and reread some text they may have missed.

 Resources

The following links are hot-linked for your convenience at http://www.sagepub .com/weinstein.

http://help.adobe.com/en_US/flash/cs/using/WSd60f23110762d6b883b18f10c b1fe1af6-7f84a.html
A more detailed introduction to manipulating the Flash timeline.

http://www.republicofcode.com/tutorials/flash/as3events/
  Additional information on event handling.

http://edutechwiki.unige.ch/en/ActionScript_3_event_handling_tutorial#List_
  of_events
  List of the most common Flash events.

http://blog.reyco1.com/method-of-removing-all-event-listeners/
  A potential method of removing all event listeners.

http://www.gavilan.edu/csis/languages/comments.html
  An interesting history of the use of comments in programming languages.

CHAPTER 4

WORKING WITH TEXT AND KEYSTROKES

IN THIS CHAPTER, YOU WILL LEARN

- About three different text field types and when to use each one
- How to set properties for text fields in the Property Inspector and from within the code
- How to change the text itself dynamically from the code
- How to format text from the code using HTML
- How to restrict text input to certain characters
- How to embed fonts for consistency across systems
- About three different systems Flash uses for processing keystrokes
- How to get the program to respond when a particular key is pressed
- How to output information about which key was pressed
- How to capture and save text entered into a text field and clear the text field

No matter what your reason for using this book (programming a complex psychological experiment, a quick questionnaire, or a lengthy survey), you will undoubtedly need to know how to present and manipulate text and how to respond to keystrokes. This seems like such an obvious requirement that it should be straightforward, so you might be surprised by the inclusion of a whole separate chapter on working with text. You will soon see, though, that there are quite a few different ways to work with text in Flash and a few factors to take into consideration when choosing from the various options available. This chapter will guide you all the way from presenting text that doesn't change (say, a set of instructions), to presenting text that you can change from within the program (say, for presenting feedback on the user's responses), to allowing users to *type in* their own text that is then processed by the program.

Note that in Flash CS5 or later you have the option to choose between two types of text editing packages: Text Layout Framework (TLF) and Classic Text. This chapter only describes how to use Classic Text. Classic Text is relatively simple to use, whereas TLF may have more flexible and extensive capabilities. Later we discuss situations in which you might want to try out TLF, but we recommend that you use the more established Classic Text as much as possible.

1. Text Field Creation

The first thing you need to do if you want to display text to the user is insert a text field into your Stage. There are two ways to insert a text field: one way creates an expandable text field, and the other creates a fixed-width text field.

> To insert an expandable text field, open the Tools Panel and click on the *Text Tool* (the icon that looks like a T). Then click anywhere on the Stage.

This creates a tiny text field just big enough to display the cursor. You can then start typing, and the text field will expand width-wise to accommodate any length of text, but text may spill off the Stage, as in the screenshot in Figure 4.1.

Figure 4.1. Expandable text field wider than the Stage. Adobe product screenshot(s) reprinted with permission from Adobe Systems Incorporated.

> To insert a fixed-width text field, click anywhere on the Stage and drag while holding down the mouse until a box of the required size appears.

This text field expands vertically instead of horizontally, as in the screen-shot in Figure 4.2.

Figure 4.2.   Fixed-width text field. Adobe product screenshot(s) reprinted with permission from Adobe Systems Incorporated.

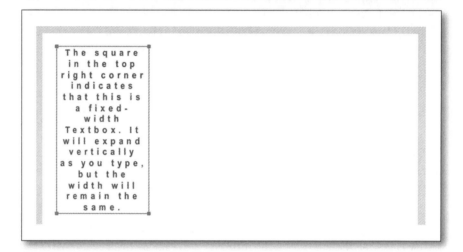

To identify what type of text field you have, click inside it and notice the symbol in the top right-hand corner: A circle indicates an expandable text field, and a square indicates a fixed-width text field, as shown in the screen-shot in Figure 4.3.

Figure 4.3.   Fixed-width and expandable text fields with their respective identifiers. Adobe product screenshot(s) reprinted with permission from Adobe Systems Incorporated.

To change an expandable text field into a fixed-width text field, drag to change the width. To change a fixed-width text field into an expandable text field, double click on the square in the top right-hand corner.

2. Types of Text Fields

The first thing you need to do is make sure that Flash is set to use Classic Text. Once you have done that, the most important thing to know about text fields is that they come in three different types: Static Text, Dynamic Text, and Input Text.

To switch from TLF to Classic Text, insert any text field and click on the Properties panel with the text field selected. Then choose "Classic Text" in the first drop-down menu. You will then be able to choose between Static Text, Dynamic Text, and Input Text in the next drop-down menu.

1) Static Text

The default setting is Static Text. This is used for text that will not (and cannot) be changed dynamically from within the code. So, whatever text you enter into a Static Text field will remain unchanged for the duration of the program and will be visible to the user as long as the particular Frame it is on is displayed.

2) Dynamic Text

You need to set the text field type to Dynamic Text if you want to change the text from within the code as the program executes. Following are examples of when you would use Dynamic Text: if you want to provide feedback that will be dependent on user input, if you want text to appear and disappear, or if you want to set different formatting throughout one text field, for instance to emphasize certain words.

To change the text type of your text field to Dynamic Text, click on the Properties Inspector with the text field selected, and select "Dynamic Text" from the drop-down menu at the top of the panel.

You will notice that a new input field appears above the text type drop-down field, labeled "Instance Name." Recall that the Instance Name is a unique name that does not belong to any other object in your Frame. Do not forget to use Instance Names that are informative and always start with the same abbreviation for each different component type. For instance, we could call our text field txtDynamicExample. In this book, all further text fields will also start with the prefix "txt."

> To give your Dynamic Text field an Instance Name, replace the placeholder text, <Instance Name>, with an appropriate name.

The advantage of Dynamic Text over Static Text is that you can use the .text method in the code to change the comments of a Dynamic Text field. To follow along with this example, make sure you have a Dynamic Text field with the Instance Name "txtDynamicExample" in your Frame. To change the contents of a Dynamic Text field, use the .text method and encompass the text you want to appear in the text field in quotation marks:

```
txtDynamicExample.text = "This text will appear
in your text field.";
```

3)   Input Text

The third text field type is Input Text. Selecting the Input Text type creates a box that the user can type into. Input Text is used when you need to allow the user to input information. Any information entered in an Input Text field can either be stored by the program for later output or used directly in the code (e.g., to provide feedback).

Input Text requires an Instance Name, just as Dynamic Text. This can be used to reference the text field in order to make it appear/disappear, save the entered text, or clear the field. This is useful for multiple trials in an experiment, where you want the user to type into the same text field on every trial.

3. Setting Text Field Properties

Clicking on Properties with a text field selected reveals all the options for customizing text fields. Table 4.1 indicates which properties can be set for each text field type (Static, Dynamic, and Input).

Table 4.1. Characteristics and relevant properties for the three text field types (Static, Dynamic, and Input Text).

Option	Static Text	Dynamic Text	Input Text
Basic Characteristics			
Text can be changed dynamically in the code	✗	✓	✓
User can type into the field	✗	✗	✓
Requires Instance Name	✗	✓	✓
Position and Size Properties			
X	✓	✓	✓
Y	✓	✓	✓
W	✓	✓	✓
H	✗	✓	✓
Lock Aspect Ratio (magnet symbol)	✓	✓	✓
Character Properties			
Family	✓	✓	✓
Style	✓	✓	✓
Size	✓	✓	✓
Letter spacing	✓	✓	✓
Color	✓	✓	✓
Auto kern	✓	✓	✓
Anti-alias	✓	✓	✓
Selectable AB	✓	✓	Always selectable
Render text as HTML	✗	✓	✓
Show border around text (icon with border)	✗	✓	✓
Toggle the superscript/subscript	Only nonselectable	✗	✗
Paragraph Properties			
Format	✓	✓	✓
Spacing	✓	✓	✓
Margins	✓	✓	✓
Behavior: Single line, Multiline, Multiline no wrap	✗	✓	✓
Behavior: Password	✗	✗	✓
Orientation	✓	✗	✗
Max chars (under Options)	✗	✗	✓

We will work from the top to the bottom of the Properties panel explaining each property in turn. Note that the Table (and the details that follow) does not include the Filters section; you can safely ignore it as it does not have a function that is useful for creating surveys and experiments. For properties that are not unique to text fields (e.g., position and size), we refer back to the previous chapter. The screenshot in Figure 4.4 shows you what the Properties panel looks like for a Dynamic Text field.

In addition to changing the properties of your text fields in the Properties panel, you can also write code to change properties while the program

Figure 4.4. Properties for Dynamic Text fields. Adobe product screenshot(s) reprinted with permission from Adobe Systems Incorporated.

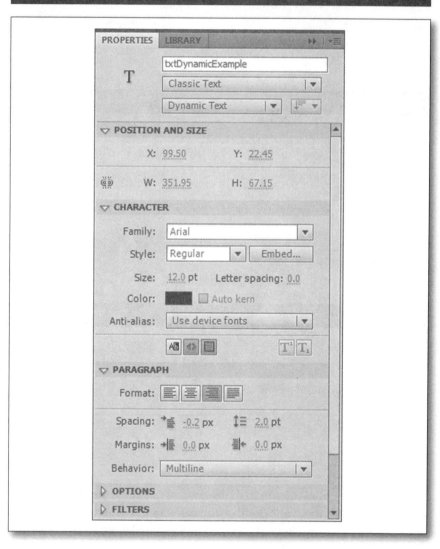

is running. For each property, we first discuss the options available in the Properties panel. Whenever it is also possible and useful to change that property from within the code, we then discuss how to do so.

1)   Position and Size

The first set of properties is Position and Size, which are the same as for Buttons. The position and size properties change automatically as you drag and resize the box on the Stage, or you can input the dimensions manually here; this is useful if you want to ensure that multiple objects are aligned and/ or proportionally sized. The magnet tool to the left of the Width allows you to indicate whether the height and width ratio (aspect ratio) should be kept constant when the text field is resized.

A note on resizing text fields: This differs depending on whether the text type is Static or Dynamic/Input. Static Text fields can only be resized horizontally, whereas Dynamic and Input Text fields can also be resized vertically. Note that no matter how you insert your text field (fixed-width or expandable), you should make the Dynamic or Input Text field big enough to hold all the text it will ever contain, or tell it to resize automatically in the code (there is no option in the Properties panel associated with this feature). To create a Dynamic/Input Text field that resizes automatically as a function of the amount of text it needs to hold, use the `.autoSize` property. You have the option to center, left-justify, or right-justify the text (replace the word "CENTER" with "LEFT" or "RIGHT").

```
    txtDynamicExample.autoSize = TextFieldAutoSize.
 CENTER
```

2)   Character

Under the Character heading are the settings that determine the look of your text. Family, Style, Size, and Color are self-explanatory. Note that these settings apply to the whole text field and cannot be applied to individual words or letters within a text field. Also, certain properties such as font and font size cannot be changed with a simple line of code, although color can be changed by calling the `.textColor` property. This is where Classic Text has some downfalls. If you want to present text with complex formatting that varies within a text field (for instance, to emphasize specific words), the easiest option is to render the text as HTML and use simple HTML tags within the code to set formatting (discussed later; note that this will not work for Static Text, which has to be formatted entirely from the Properties panel).

To the right of the Style drop-down field is a button that says **Embed...** . This allows you to "embed" fonts in your .swf file so that they can be used every time the program runs, instead of trying to pull fonts from the user's system. This ensures presentation consistency, but you trade off on file size as embedding fonts significantly increases the size of the final .swf file. If you choose not to embed fonts, you need to select **Use device fonts** in the Anti-alias drop-down field (discussed later). In this case, the font that you have chosen will only render correctly if that font is installed on the user's system. If the font is not installed on the system, a different font will be chosen in its place. This could create various problems: text not fitting into the field, line breaks in the wrong place, and having no way of making sure that each user sees the same thing (crucial if you are using a text field to present word stimuli in a psychology experiment or a set of questions in a survey). We thus strongly recommend that you choose to embed fonts.

To bring up the font embedding window (see Figure 4.5), click on the Properties panel with a text field selected and click on *Character* → *Embed. . . .* Then choose the font and font style you want to embed, and give your font a unique name. Select all the character ranges you want to be able to present, and add any additional special characters in the box below. To embed another font, click on the + icon above the font list on the left panel of the dialog box.

Figure 4.5.   Font embedding menu. Adobe product screenshot(s) reprinted with permission from Adobe Systems Incorporated.

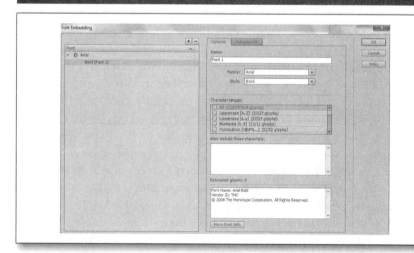

Embedding only the necessary characters will greatly cut down on the size of your file. However, make sure that every single character you want to display is embedded, because any character that is not embedded will not appear on the screen when the program is loaded by the user. Notice that in the Character Ranges menu, the category "All" consists of a thousand or more glyphs (this will vary depending on which font you are embedding), whereas you probably only need capital letters, lowercase letters, numerals, and punctuation (a little over 100 glyphs). There is also a box below the menu where you can enter any additional characters to be embedded (***Also include these characters***). Another important point is that if you want to use the same font in a different style (italics, bold), that style needs to be embedded as a different font.

Under Letter spacing you can change the distance between characters, to make them closer (negative value) or further apart (positive value). The default is 0, and the range is -60 (letters are right on top of each other) to +60 (letters look like they have approximately 10 spaces between them).

Auto-kern determines the way spaces between certain character combinations are handled. Leaving it on means that some character combinations will have adjusted spacing, whereas turning it off will lead to uniform spacing between all character combinations. This is an aesthetic choice for you to make (see Resources for an article about kerning).

The Anti-alias options also determine how your text is displayed (anti-alias is a type of smoothing that makes characters appear rounder and easier to read). You can read up on the different Anti-alias options elsewhere (see Resources), but since you will mostly be using text fields to display normal text (as opposed to animation), we suggest you stick with ***Anti-alias for readability***. The T^1 and T_1 icons turn selected text into superscript and subscript, respectively.

The three icons below the Anti-alias options (see Figure 4.4) allow you to set whether text is selectable, whether it is displayed as HTML, and whether there is a border around the text field. Using the ▓▓ icon lets you determine whether the text field is selectable, in which case the user can highlight the text on the screen (for instance, so that the user can copy and paste it into another program). Note that Input Text is always by definition selectable, since the user can click on the field and type.

```
//Turn selectability of a text field on and off;
txtDynamicExample.selectable = true;
txtDynamicExample.selectable = false;
```

For Dynamic and Input Text only, the icon with angle brackets  allows you to render text as HTML. This is useful if you want to vary formatting within the text field. You can include HTML tags when you set the text to appear in the text field from within the code. There are some limitations to the HTML tags you can use, so stick to the basics and check the Resources for a link to a longer list of tags and general information on HTML. Generally, though, you can use HTML tags to change the font, font size, color, and style, as well as indicate line and paragraph breaks. We do not cover HTML tags in detail here, but following are a few of the most common tags and an example showing how to add them to your text. To use HTML tags in your Dynamic Text field, first click on the angled brackets symbol in the Properties panel to enable HTML text for a text field. Then use the `.htmlText` method instead of the standard `.text` method to set text from the code. HTML tags are included within the text you want to display.

```
txtDynamicExample.htmlText = '<b>Bold text </b><u>Underlined text </u>';

txtDynamicExample.htmlText += '<font color="#CC0000">Red text </font>';

txtDynamicExample.htmlText += '<font size = "36">Huge text </font>';
```

Note that the "+=" operator appends additional text to whatever is already in the text field. The "=" operator would clear any previous text and replace it with the new text. The screenshot in Figure 4.6 shows how the HTML text will render when you run your program.

Figure 4.6. Various HTML formatting styles. Adobe product screenshot(s) reprinted with permission from Adobe Systems Incorporated.

Another property you can only set for Dynamic and Input Text fields is to show a border around the text by clicking on the border icon ▤. The border can also be turned on and off from the code.

```
//Turning a text field border on and off;

txtDynamicExample.border = true;

txtDynamicExample.border = false;
```

Finally, on the far right you can toggle superscript T^1 and subscript T_1 fonts, which can only be applied to individual characters in a nonselectable Static Text field.

3) Paragraph

The properties in the Paragraph section should all be self-explanatory if you are familiar with standard word processing conventions. Classic Text also gives you the freedom to create vertical text fields (under the Orientation property), break text apart into individual characters that can be moved around the Stage, and convert characters into shapes, but we will stick to the basics of standard, horizontal text. If you want to find out about more creative text uses, consult the Resources section for help on how to do this using Classic Text, or play with the TLF.

For Dynamic and Input Text only, under the Paragraph subsection of the Properties panel, the Behavior drop-down field is now activated, and you can choose whether the text in your Dynamic Text field displays on one line (Single line), on multiple lines with automatic word wrap fitted to the width of your text field (Multiline), or on multiple lines but without automatic word wrap (i.e., you will have to indicate line breaks in the code; Multiline no wrap). Probably the most commonly used behavior for our purposes is Multiline.

For Input Text only, if you would like users to be able to input information confidentially, you can use the Password Behavior for Input Text. This makes all characters appear as asterisks on the screen when typed. The actual typed characters can be saved and used in the code, however. An Input Text field can acquire Password Behavior from the code too.

```
txtInputExample.displayAsPassword = true;

txtInputExample.displayAsPassword = false;
```

You can also restrict the number of characters that can be typed into the text field by the user, by changing the "Max chars" property under Options (.maxChars; the default option is 0, which means no limit). From within the code, you can also restrict the type of characters the user can input into a text field. You can also prevent certain characters from being entered by using the ^ symbol.

```
//To restrict the number of characters;

txtDynamicExample.maxChars = 12;

//To restrict input to lowercase letters;

txtDynamicExample.restrict = "a-z";

//To restrict input to a range of digits;

txtDynamicExample.restrict = "1-9";

/*To restrict input to specific letters or
numbers*/

txtDynamicExample.restrict = "abc123";

/* The following code does not allow lowercase
characters to be input*/

txtDynamicExample.restrict = "^a-z";
```

When you use an Input Text field, you may naturally want the program to save any text entered by the user. We do not cover this here, but instead see "Chapter 7: Condition Assignment and Randomization" for how to save Input Text.

4. Other Ways of Working With Text in Flash

Earlier we briefly covered three main approaches to editing text in Flash:

- Using the Property Inspector to set overall characteristics for the text field
- Using commands in the code to change properties of dynamic/input text fields
- Using HTML text to format text from within the code

These are only a few options, and they should be sufficient to fulfill your requirements, but if you want to try something more advanced, here are some more options:

1) Creating a TextFormat object in the code and applying it to your text field (to set properties that are not direct properties of the text field itself, such as font). The advantage of this method over HTML text is that there are no messy tags to include in the text, so in your code you can see the text as it will be displayed to the user.

2) Creating new text fields from within the code rather than by drawing it on the Stage.

3) Using Cascading Style Sheets (CSS) instead of HTML tags. This is more advanced and probably only useful if you are collaborating with website designers or other web professionals.

4) Using TLF instead of Classic Text. This opens up a whole new world of formatting opportunities, but it is only recommended if you are working with complicated layouts (think newspaper-style columns or busy website designs) and need complete control over every aspect of text in your project.

5. Key Recognition

This section deals with everything you need to know about responding to user input. You already know how to make Flash respond to a button press, but here you also learn how to make the program respond when the user presses different keys and how to save text input by the user into a text field. The first thing you need to know is how ActionScript processes and interprets keystrokes. There are three systems by which ActionScript categories and recognizes keys: key codes (`keyCode`), character codes (`charCode`), and constant values.

1) The `keyCode` is a numerical value that refers to the physical key on the keyboard, regardless of which character the user intended to generate; for instance, regardless of whether you type a 5 or a % symbol, the same `keyCode` is activated.

2) The `charCode` is also a numerical value, but it relates to the actual character, which can be typed by different keys (for instance, numbers can be typed either from the row above the letters or from the number keypad on the right of some keyboards).

3) Some of the more important keys (e.g., ENTER, SPACE) also have "constant values" that can be used instead of the `keyCode`. This is important because `keyCode` mappings may differ from computer to computer, whereas the constant values will always refer to the relevant key. So, wherever possible, you should use the constant values. Check the Resources for a link to the full list of keys that have constants, but here is a short list of the most common keys:

```
Keyboard.BACKSPACE

Keyboard.DELETE

Keyboard.ENTER

Keyboard.ESCAPE

Keyboard.SPACE
```

You can look up the `keyCodes` and `charCodes` for any keys you want to use in the program by checking the links in the Resources, but see the "Looking up keyCodes and charCodes" section that follows for instructions on how to use code in your program to look up these values.

Example: Responding to a Keystroke

In order to try out a program that responds to keystrokes within the Flash interface, after you compile it you must disable keyboard shortcuts, otherwise keystrokes will not register. This only applies to testing the program from within Flash—the keystrokes would register if you ran the program in a Flash player.

To disable keyboard shortcuts, compile the program and go to *Control* → *Disable Keyboard Shortcuts* in the window of the compiled program.

The first thing we need to do to make our program respond to a keystroke is add an event listener, just as we did when we wanted the program to respond to a button press. This time, the event listener is listening out for a different category of events, so we use a different class of events: `KeyboardEvent`. We can add the event listener directly to the Stage or to specific components. To follow along with this example, add an Input Text field to your Stage and give it the Instance Name "txtInput."

```
    /*The following event listener calls the function
"processResponse" when a key is pressed in "txtInput"*/

    txtInput.addEventListener(KeyboardEvent.KEY_
DOWN, processResponse);
```

You have two options in terms of when the function associated with the event listener will execute: either as soon as the key is pressed or when the key is released, in which case you need to use the .KEY_UP event instead of .KEY_DOWN. The distinction between KEY_UP and KEY_DOWN is unimportant unless you are particularly interested in measuring reaction times, but it is crucial if you are (see Chapter 8 on timers for more information).

To test that your program is registering keystrokes, add the following function, which traces a message to indicate that a key was pressed.

```
    /*This function traces a message to indicate
that the keypress event was registered.*/

    function processResponse(evt:KeyboardEvent):void

    {

        trace("a key was pressed");

    }
```

Example: Looking up keyCodes and charCodes

Aside from looking up keyCode and charCode values in tables, the easiest way to figure them out is to write code that will bring up that information for any key you strike. The following code will trace the keyCode, charCode, and the actual character in response to a keystroke. Use the program from the previous example, and put the following code within the function that executes when a keystroke is registered ("processResponse").

```
    /*Output the keyCode associated with the key
pressed*/

    trace("keyCode:", evt.keyCode)
```
                                        Box (Continued)

```
Box (Continued)

    /*Output the charCode associated with the key
pressed*/

    trace("charCode:", evt.charCode)

    /*Output the actual character associated with
the key pressed*/

    trace("Actual character:", String.fromCharCode
(evt.charCode))
```

The first two lines should be self-explanatory; in the third line, we translate the charCode to a String that contains the actual character it refers to, using the .fromCharCode method. If you save this program, you can use it as a handy tool whenever you need to know a charCode or keyCode.

Example: Responding to Specific Keys

Next, you need to know how to specify different behaviors for different keys. That is, you might only want the contents of the function to execute if a particular key is pressed. For instance, you might have a task that requires participants to press one of two keys to indicate their responses (e.g., Y to indicate yes and N to indicate no). Alternatively, you might tell participants to hit SPACE to proceed to the next screen. To make your function respond only to certain keys, you will need to know the keyCode, charCode or constant value related to the key you want the program to respond to, and then you will need to write a conditional statement that specifies which keys should elicit which response.

In the following example, the function we used for our previous example is extended to output a special message when either Y, N, or SPACE is pressed. To follow along with this example, use the project from the previous example and add the following code to the function that responds to your keystroke ("processResponse").

```
    //if y or Y is pressed output "yes";

    if(evt.keyCode == 89){trace ("yes")}

    //if n or N is pressed output "no";
```

```
    else if(evt.keyCode == 78){trace ("no")}

    //if SPACE is pressed output "SPACE";

    else  if(evt.keyCode  ==  Keyboard.SPACE){trace
("SPACE")}
```

Example: Capturing Input Text

Another thing you will need to know how to do is capture and save text input by a user into a text field. In the next example, we write a function that saves the contents of a text field to a variable and clears the text field when the user presses ENTER. To follow along with this example, you need to start a new project and take the following steps:

1) Add an Input Text field to your Stage and give it the Instance Name "txtInput."

2) Define a String variable called "savedText."

3) Write an event listener that listens for a KEY_DOWN keyboard event on the txtInput field and calls a function called "processInputText."

As we want to save the contents of the text field only when the user presses ENTER, we need to enclose the statements in our function within a conditional statement.

```
    function processInputText(evt:KeyboardEvent):void

    {

        //Check whether the key pressed was ENTER;

        if (evt.keyCode == Keyboard.ENTER)

            {

        /*Pass the text currently in the text field
to the variable*/

                savedText = txtInput.text;

        //Clear the contents of the text field;
                                    Box (Continued)
```

```
Box (Continued)
                    txtInput.text="";

         //Send the contents of the variable to output;
                    trace(savedText);

             }

      }
```

Exercise: Look at Figure 4.7 and try to recreate the way the text is formatted using any combination of HTML text, code, and options from the Properties panel.

Figure 4.7.   Screenshot of a compiled program showing formatted text. Adobe product screenshot(s) reprinted with permission from Adobe Systems Incorporated.

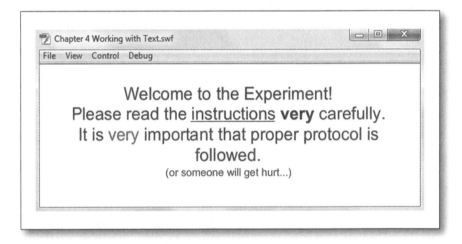

In this chapter, you learned that Static Text is used to present text that does not change, Dynamic Text is used to present text that needs to be changed dynamically from the code, and Input Text is used when you want to allow users to enter their own text. You learned to set properties for the text fields both in the Property Inspector and from within the code by calling the relevant properties. You also learned how to change the contents of a text field presented to the user directly from the code. In order to change the way the text appears, you used HTML formatting code. To ensure that your text appeared the same across all computer systems, you learned to embed fonts in your program. You also learned to restrict Input Text fields to specific characters. This is useful if you want to ask the user questions such as "How many times per week do you work on your Flash exercises?" and you want a numeric response.

Moving on to keystrokes, you learned that Flash classifies keystrokes in terms of keyCodes, charCodes, and constant values. You used these codes to get the program to react to the press of a specific key. Of course, in order to get Flash to respond to a keystroke in the first place, you used an event listener—either one that listened for the key to be pressed or one that listened for the key to be released. You also learned to output information about which key was pressed, based on keyCodes or charCodes. Finally, you learned how to save text from an Input Text field and clear it, ready for the next response.

At this juncture, we hope that the necessity of knowing how to work with text is evident: Displaying and styling text on the screen is the foundation of instructions, surveys, and certain experimental stimuli (e.g., words and sentences). Likewise, collecting data entered by keyboard is fundamental, too. In just the last two chapters, you have learned all the tools necessary to, for example, program an entire questionnaire consisting of short answer questions.

Resources

The following links are hot-linked for your convenience at http://www .sagepub.com/weinstein.

http://gskinner.com/blog/archives/2010/07/some_thoughts_o.html
    Some thoughts on TLF.

http://help.adobe.com/en_US/flash/cs/using/WSd60f23110762d6b883b18f10c
    b1fe1af6-7d29a.html#WSd60f23110762d6b883b18f10cb1fe1af6-7d22a
    Setting Classic Text properties (including anti-aliasing options).

http://help.adobe.com/en_US/incopy/cs/using/WSa285fff53dea4f8617383751
    001ea8cb3f-6e14a.html
    An article about kerning.

http://www.w3.org/TR/html/
>   General information on HTML.

http://www.designscripting.com/2010/08/html-tags-supported-by-flash/
>   List of HTML tags supported by Flash.

http://html-color-codes.com/
>   HTML color codes.

http://www.signar.se/blog/as-3-charcodes/
>   charCode and keyCode reference.

http://help.adobe.com/en_US/FlashPlatform/reference/actionscript/3/flash/
ui/Keyboard.html#constantSummary
>   Definitive list of constant keyCodes.

http://coding.smashingmagazine.com/2011/01/11/keeping-web-users-safe-by-
sanitizing-input-data/
>   The importance of sanitizing database input.

http://help.adobe.com/en_US/as3/dev/WS5b3ccc516d4fbf351e63e3d118a
9b90204-7d01.html
>   Additional information on capturing keyboard input.

CHAPTER **5**

PRESENTING AND STORING INFORMATION IN ARRAYS

IN THIS CHAPTER, YOU WILL LEARN

- When you might need to use an array and when to use it instead of other variable types
- How to create an array and define its contents
- How to cycle through an array from start to finish
- How to add elements to an array from user input
- How to find out if something is an element in your array, and if so, then at which index it is located

1. What Is an Array and When Would You Need to Use It?

In Chapter 2 on ActionScript basics, you learned that there are different types of variables that you can use to store and present information. Each type of variable you have encountered so far (e.g., `int`, `Number`, `String`, `Boolean`) can store one piece of information at a time. In many situations, it is helpful to use a variable that stores multiple pieces of information at a time. For instance, imagine you want to present the user with a list of words.

You could assign each word to a different variable (e.g., `String` variables named "word1," "word2," "word3," etc.), but this would involve creating as many variables as the number of words you wanted to present. Instead of wasting time on such an inefficient procedure, you can use a different type of variable, an `Array`, which can store multiple items at once.

Arrays are like numbered lists that allow you to access any item in the list by its index. Examples of when you might want to use an array include the following: presenting a set of consecutive questions, presenting a list of words, and presenting a series of pictures. The rule of thumb is that in all cases where you want to store information as a list, you should use arrays instead of any other type of variable. Arrays become particularly essential when you want to present items in different orders in different versions of the program. You can also use arrays if you need to set up a list of usernames and associated passwords for different users to be able to log on to a program you write. An array of usernames and an analogous array of passwords would permit you to match the two in order to check whether the information entered is correct (see Figure 5.1).

Figure 5.1. Diagram of username and password arrays.

...	27	28	29	30	31	32	...	index
...	User27	User28	User29	User30	User31	User32	...	**Username Array**
...	G6C4yE	s5uMA4	jaqa6U	Baqe5r	2huDa9	WEje3P	...	**Password Array**

 ## 2. Defining and Populating Arrays

To start using an `Array` variable, you need to define it and populate it with "elements" (i.e., the items on your list). There are various ways to write this in the code.

```
/*Define a new Array just like you define any
new variable*/

var listOfItems:Array = new Array;
```

```
    /*If the elements in your Array are short, you
can add them all to the Array in one line.*/

    listOfItems = ["one", "two", "three", "four",
"five"];

    /*If the elements in your Array are longer, you
can define each element on a separate line.*/

    listOfItems[0] = "This is the first element of
your array, but it has an index of 0";

    listOfItems[1] = "This is the second element
of your array, but it has an index of 1";

    listOfItems[2] = "This is the third element of
your array, but it has an index of 2";

    listOfItems[3] = "This is the fourth element
of your array, but it has an index of 3";

    listOfItems[4] = "This is the fifth element of
your array, but it has an index of 4";
```

An important thing to note about the Array variable in Flash is that the first index of the Array is not 1, but 0. Although this may be nonintuitive (since you are probably used to starting your lists from 1), it is best to get into the habit of using index 0 for the first item of your array, as skipping it could cause problems when you try to manipulate the array later on.

Note that unlike other variables, the Array does not have a prespecified data type (e.g., numerical/text). The data type of each element is determined on an item-by-item basis depending on the formatting you use. That is, you can enter two or more different data types into an Array. If you want to add a text element (i.e., when you would normally use a String variable if you only had one piece of information) into your array, make sure you use quote marks, otherwise Flash will think you are trying to call a variable and you will receive an error message. If you want to add a numerical value to your array (i.e., when you would normally use an int or Number variable type), make sure the value is not in quote marks if you want Flash to treat it as a number instead of as text.

3. Properties and Methods of Arrays

The `Array` variable only has one property: length. To find out the length of your array at any time, simply trace the name of your array followed by `.length`.

```
/*This line traces the length of the Array
called "listOfItems"*/

    trace(listOfItems.length);
```

Note that the length of the array is determined automatically by referencing the highest index of the items in your array. That is, if you define a new array and add just one item in the fifth index (e.g., `listOfItems[5] = "item 6"`), the `.length` property will be set to 6 (recall that the Array starts from 0). Figure 5.2 shows the contents of your array once you have added an item to the fifth index.

Figure 5.2.   Contents and length of an array after adding one item at index 5.

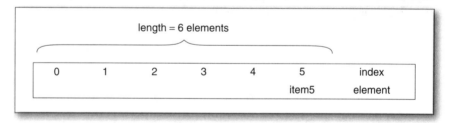

The length property is very useful when manipulating arrays. If you want to cycle through all the elements in your array, for instance to present a list of words, you would need a way of knowing that you have reached the end of the array. The `.length` property will tell you that (see the following example). Arrays can also be manipulated by various methods. Here are the two most useful methods, which we put into practice in the following examples:

`.push` appends any content specified to a new element in the next empty index. The syntax for this method is as follows:

```
ArrayName.push("information to be pushed into a
new element");
```

For instance, if you have an array of 11 elements [indices 0-10] and you use the `.push` method, a new element will be created with an index of 11. We use this method for storing responses entered by the user (see the example: Cycling Through an Array From Start to Finish).

`.indexOf` searches for any information you specify within your array and returns the index of the element that contains your search query. The syntax for this method is as follows:

```
ArrayName.indexOf("search query");
```

You will need to use this method for the following exercise, where your task is to create arrays of logins and matched passwords.

Example: Cycling Through an Array From Start to Finish

Once you define an `Array` variable, it is easy to write code to cycle through the array sequentially. This is conceptually similar to the function you used to navigate from Frame to Frame in Chapter 3.

To follow along with this example, you need to take the following preliminary steps, all of which should be familiar to you by now. Following is a discussion of the function that cycles through each item in the array.

1) Add a Dynamic Text field to your Stage and give it the Instance Name "txtQuestion."

2) Add a Button to your Stage and give it the Instance Name "btnNextQuestion."

3) Add an to your code that listens out for a mouse click on "btnNextQuestion" and calls the function "presentNextQuestion."

4) Define an array called "listOfQuestions" with a different question in each of indices 0 through 5.

5) Define an integer variable (`int`) called "i" for use as a counter.

6) Assign "i" the initial value of 0.

The "presentNextItem" function does the following:

1) It checks to see if there are any elements left to present by using the .length property of the Array variable and stops cycling through the array if it has been exhausted.

2) If there are no elements left in the array, it presents a message to indicate the end of the list.

3) If there are elements left in the array, it loads the next element in the "listOfQuestions" array into "txtQuestion" by using the counter variable "i" as an index.

4) It adds 1 to the counter variable "i."

```
/*This function is executed when the user clicks
"btnNextQuestion."*/

function presentNextQuestion(evt:MouseEvent):void

{

/*Check to see if there are any elements left
in the array. If there are no elements left in the
array, the counter "i" is equal to the length of
the array.*/

if(i == listOfQuestions.length)

    {

        /*If there are no elements left, present
a message*/

        txtQuestion.text = "End of list";

    }

    else

    {

        /*If there are elements left, present
the element stored in index "i."*/

        txtQuestion.text = listOfQuestions[i];
```

```
        //Add 1 to the counter;

        i++;

    }

}
```

What does this function do? The first part of the function checks whether the end of the array has been reached. That is, the `if` statement checks whether the counter "i" that is keeping track of where we are in the array is equal to the length of the array. If the counter has reached the length of the array, this means that there are no elements left to present. If this condition is met, "txtQuestion" shows the message "End of list."

Otherwise (`else`), the Text Field "txtQuestion" is populated with the element stored in the index that is equal to the current value of the counter variable "i." Finally, after the element is loaded into the text field, 1 is added to the counter variable "i" so that it updates and the next item from the array is presented when the function is next executed.

Of course, you will not always want to cycle through an array from beginning to end in the same order. Often, you might prefer to cycle through an array in a different random order for each user. Instructions for how to do this appear in Chapter 7 where we cover randomization.

Example: Dynamically Manipulating Arrays: Storing Responses

Arrays are a useful tool for storing inputs from participants that are gathered during an experiment or survey. You can easily add to and remove from arrays while the program is running. It makes more sense to use an `Array` variable rather than other variable types that can only hold one piece of information at a time to store participant responses, because usually you have multiple responses to save from each phase of your survey or experiment.

Imagine you are presenting participants with a list of questions and asking them to make a response to each question. You would like to store these responses in an array and be able to match up the responses to the questions. An easy way to do this is to have a counter that tracks what index number you are on in your array of questions, and use this same counter to index the responses. After each question is answered, you can capture the contents of an Input Text field and add it as a new element to an array. The index of the new element of each trial is defined by the counter.

To make this work, we have to add another function to the previous example. The new function is executed only once: when the user clicks on the Button for the first time to view the first question. This is because we want something different to occur on subsequent questions: We want to store the response to the question that had just been presented. To follow along with this example, use the project from the previous example and take the following steps:

1) Add an Input Text field to your Stage and give it the Instance Name "txtAnswer."

2) Define a new array called "listOfAnswers."

3) Delete the EventListener associated with "btnNextQuestion" and the function "presentNextQuestion."

4) Add an EventListener to the Button "btnNextQuestion" that calls the function "presentFirstQuestion."

We will now write two functions—one called "presentFirstQuestion" for loading the first question and the other called "presentNextQuestion" for storing the response and presenting the next question.

```
/*This function is executed only the first time
the user clicks "btnNextQuestion."*/

function presentFirstQuestion(evt:MouseEvent):
void

    {

        txtQuestion.text = listOfQuestions[i];

        btnNextQuestion.removeEventListener(Mouse
Event.CLICK, presentFirstQuestion);

        btnNextQuestion.addEventListener(Mouse
Event.CLICK, presentNextQuestion);

    }

/*This function is executed when the user
clicks "btnNextQuestion" after the first time.*/

function presentNextQuestion(evt:MouseEvent):void
```

```
{

    //Store the response currently in "txtAnswer";

    listOfAnswers[i] = txtAnswer.text;

    //Clear "txtAnswer";

    txtAnswer.text = "";

    //Add 1 to the counter;

    i++;

//Present the element stored in index "i";

if(i == listOfQuestions.length)

    {

        txtQuestion.text = "End of list";

        //Output all the questions and answers;

for (i = 0; i <listOfQuestions.length; i++)

{

  trace(i, listOfQuestions[i], listOfAnswers[i]);

}

    }

    /*If there are more elements left, present the
element stored in index "i."*/

        else{txtQuestion.text = listOfQuestions[i];}

    }
```

You might be wondering what the `for` loop that executes at the end of the list does. Starting at zero and stopping when it gets to the end of the "listOfQuestions" array, for each index it traces the index and then the question and response stored in that index of the "listOfQuestions" and "listOfAnswers" arrays, respectively.

Example: Looking up Information in an Array

Another useful thing you can do with arrays is look up the position of any element in the array or determine whether a given element exists in an array. For instance, let us say you ask the user to list his or her top five favorite cities in order from 1 to 5, and you store the responses in an array. Now you would like to know whether London is in the user's top five, and if so, where it is located on the list. Instead of checking each of the five elements of the response array sequentially to see if they contain the String "London," you can use the `.indexOf` method to determine whether the element "London" exists in that array.

To follow along with this example, you can use your previous project. Once all five questions have been answered, we will search the responses to see if one of them is "London." Simply add the following code to the part of the function that executes once the end of the list has been reached.

```
/*Return the index of the element in which the
exact string "London" resides.*/

trace(listOfAnswers.indexOf("London"));
```

If the String you are looking for is an element in the referenced array, the trace statement will return the relevant index. If the String is not an element in the array, the trace statement will return the value -1. There are two important things to note here: First, this method uses the "strict equality" rule and will only return an index if the search term is identical to the element in the array, including the data type. For instance, if you have the Number 132 in your array but search for the String "132," the `.indexOf` method will return -1. Do not forget that ActionScript is case sensitive, so searching for "Cassidy" will not find a match in "cassidy." Second, the array is searched forward from the beginning (starting from the 0 index), and the search stops when a matching element is located, so if you have multiple elements that match your search term, you will get the lowest index.

There are various other methods you might find useful when manipulating arrays, such as pushing and splicing if you want to insert elements at different indices in your array or sort the array according to various criteria (e.g., alphabetically). You can find more information about these methods by following the links in the Resources section.

4. Common Array Malfunctions

The array is one of the most powerful tools in Flash, but it can also be one of the trickiest to master. Arrays, especially when used in conjunction with logical loops, are prone to bugs, despite a programmer's best intentions. One of the most common errors when using arrays is trying to access an index that does not exist. This can be triggered by a static line of code, but it can also stem from an incorrectly constructed loop. Being "off by one" can also cause array errors. This issue arises when the code iterates through an array, for example, incorrectly starting at the second array element or attempting to end one element past the length of the array (`array.length + 1`). Additional problems are sometimes caused when the programmer thinks the array contains one type of element (say, an integer) when in reality it contains another (a `String`).

As such, it is recommended that you occasionally trace the contents of your arrays to the screen, especially when you are using more complicated code structures (e.g., nested loops). A pen or pencil can sometimes be a useful "analog" way of tracking contents of an array as well. Whenever your program does not seem to be working even when you think it should, arrays in loops are the first place to check. Make sure all the logical operators (e.g., > or &&) are in the right place, you are calling the array elements you intend, and the array actually contains the elements you believe it does. If you are careful when constructing and manipulating arrays, many of these potential problems will be minimized.

Exercise: Write a program that allows users to log on with a unique login and password and outputs "success" or "failure," depending on whether the login and password match. To do this, make up a list of login and password combinations. Create a Frame with two Input Text fields, one for the login and the other for the password. Add a Button that executes a function to test whether the entered login and password match.

Hint: Create two separate arrays, one for the logins and one for the passwords. Use matching indices to pair the logins with the appropriate passwords (this is called "parallel arrays"). Use the `.indexOf` method to locate the login and check whether the element in the same index in the password array matches the entered password.

In this chapter, you learned that the array is a basic data type of Flash and a building block of the programming language. You also learned about its direct conceptual applications to experiments or surveys you may want to program. Arrays are used to store lists of information, and anything that can be thought of as a list—participant numbers, stimuli to present, alphabetized responses, or final data, to name a few—will need to be stored in an array. You learned how to define an array and populate it with elements, how to cycle through these elements, and how to change which elements form part of the array. You also learned how to query your array in order to locate a particular element or find the element at a particular index. This technique is useful if you want to compare the contents of an element with some other information, for instance, when checking a password or the accuracy of a response. We return briefly to arrays in Chapter 7, where we learn how to randomize them.

 ## Resources

The following links are hot-linked for your convenience at http://www .sagepub.com/weinstein.

http://help.adobe.com/en_US/FlashPlatform/reference/actionscript/3/Array .html
  The API entry for the Array object.

http://www.republicofcode.com/tutorials/flash/as3arrays/
  A simple introduction to Arrays.

http://www.onebyonedesign.com/tutorials/array_methods/
  A list of advanced Array methods.

http://www.smartwebby.com/Flash/external_data.asp
  Loading data from external text files into Flash. Pair with Arrays to save lots of time!

QUESTIONNAIRE TOOLS

- How to present questions and response options in the form of a drop-down list, radio buttons, or check boxes
- How to allow the user to continue only once a question has been answered
- How to store the selected response option(s)
- How to use a slider to allow responses on a continuous scale

In this chapter, we learn about the tools Flash offers for creating attractive questionnaires. We learn how to allow the user to select answers by choosing from a drop-down list, clicking radio buttons, and ticking check boxes. To help you choose which of the three presentation formats fits the type of question you want to present, use the flowchart in Figure 6.1.

Lists, RadioButtons, and CheckBoxes are components in Flash, and they can be found in the Components panel. To access this window if it is not already on your workspace, go to *Window → Components*, or select *Ctrl+F7*.

Figure 6.1. Choosing the appropriate component for questionnaire design.

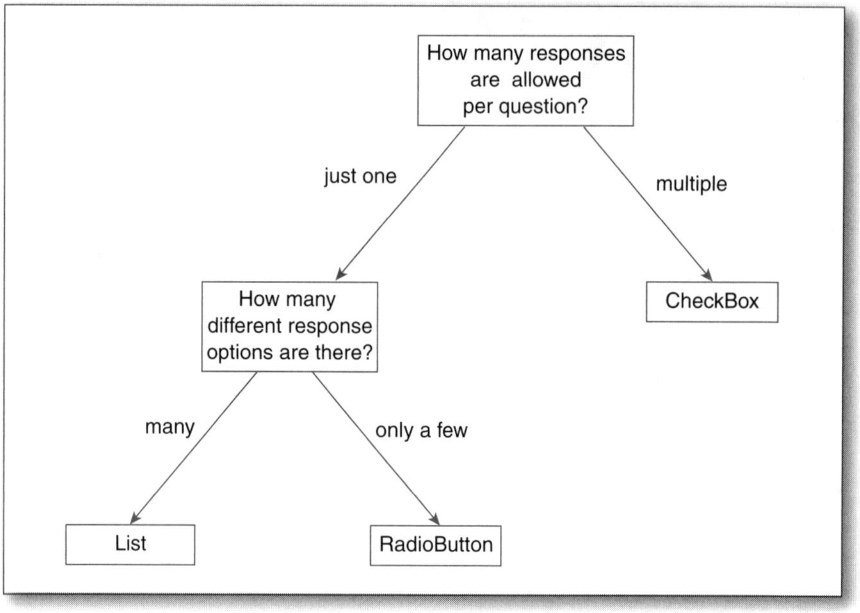

How many responses are allowed per question?

just one

multiple

How many different response options are there?

CheckBox

many

only a few

List

RadioButton

 ## 1. List Component

A List component is commonly referred to as a "drop-down menu" and is familiar to anyone who uses a computer on a regular basis. When a user clicks on a List, the complete set of possible responses is displayed on-screen. The user selects a given response from the List to indicate his or her choice.

> To add a List to a Frame, drag a List component from the Components window to your Stage.

Dragging the List component onto your Stage creates a square. This will look quite different once you actually compile the program, but unfortunately, on your Stage it will always appear just as an outline with a circle in the middle. Editing the visual properties of components is extremely complicated, because each feature of the component (for a List, e.g., the scroll bar) is edited separately and has multiple layers. We advise you not to alter these properties for now. If you accidentally find yourself in Component Editing mode (double-clicking the square on your Stage will do that), click on "Scene 1" just above your Stage to return to normal view. The first thing you need to do with a new List is, of course, give it an Instance Name. For a List, we can use the prefix "lst" in our Instance Name. Next, we can set some parameters for this component.

> To set the parameters, click on the Properties panel while the box on your Stage is selected. The parameters we will be dealing with are listed under Component Parameters. Note: for Flash CS5 or earlier, parameters are listed in the Component Inspector, a separate panel.

You will see the following parameters:

`allowMultipleSelection` determines whether the user can select multiple responses to one question. Sometimes it is useful to be able to select multiple entries in a List, if more than one answer applies to a question. However, the CheckBox component is generally more useful in such situations (see the flowchart in Figure 6.1), so we will work with single selections only. Leave the box next to this parameter unchecked.

`dataProvider` can be used to define the elements in your List if you do not want to change them from the code. See the following section on adding elements to a List component for instructions on how to do this.

`enabled` determines whether the List component can be accessed by the user. This box should be checked, otherwise the List will appear grayed out when the Frame loads. This parameter is useful if you want to prevent the user from being able to access a component until an event has occurred. Figure 6.2 shows the appearance of two Lists, one of which has not been enabled.

`horizontalLineScrollSize` determines the amount of content in pixels that is scrolled, horizontally (left/right), when a scroll arrow is clicked. Horizontal scrolling is only useful if you have elements in a List that do not fit in the component—this is inadvisable. Set this parameter higher if your List items are very long.

`horizontalPageScrollSize` determines the amount of content in pixels that is scrolled, horizontally, when you click inside the scroll bar.

Figure 6.2. Appearance of enabled and disabled List components in an uncompiled program. Adobe product screenshot(s) reprinted with permission from Adobe Systems Incorporated.

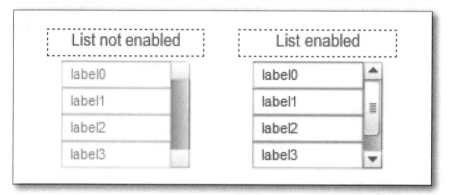

Leaving it at 0 means it will automatically set the scroll rate to match the width of your List.

`verticalLineScrollSize` determines the amount of content that is scrolled, in pixels, vertically (up/down), when a scroll arrow is clicked. If you have many elements in your List, they will not fit in your component. Set this parameter higher if your List has many elements.

`verticalPageScrollSize` determines the amount of content that is scrolled, in pixels, vertically, when you click inside the scroll bar.

`horizontalScrollPolicy/verticalScrollPolicy` determines whether there is a scroll bar available (on/off/auto). Leaving this parameter set to "auto" means that there will only be a scroll bar if there is content that does not fit into the dimensions of the component.

`visible` determines whether the component appears when the Frame loads. Unchecking this box will render the component invisible when the Frame loads.

```
    /*Change parameters from within the code by
calling the appropriate parameter after the Instance
Name of the List.*/

    lstResponses.visible = true;

    lstResponses.horizontalScrollPolicy = "off";
```

Once you have created your List component, you need to define the elements that will appear in the List. Each element in a List component has two parameters: label and data. The label parameter defines what shows up on the screen, and the data parameter is used to give each response a code. For instance, the actual response options shown to the user could be long sentences, whereas the data would be just a keyword for each response option or a numerical index that represents each response. This can be useful if you want to use a shorthand in your output instead of outputting long items or if you want to code one particular response as the correct response. That is, you could give all responses except the correct response a data parameter of 0.

Example: Using a List to Present Response Options

To follow along with the example, do the following:

1) Drag an instance of the List component to your Stage.

2) Resize it to 300 x 100 pixels.

3) Give your List the Instance Name "lstResponses."

There are two ways of adding elements to a List: through the `dataProvider` property or in the code. In some cases, you may want to reuse your List component to display different sets of response options on the same Frame, in which case you would need to define the elements in the code. If you are creating a List that you do not need to edit later, however, you can add elements to the List using a simple dialog box in the `dataProvider` parameter.

> To add elements to a List through the dataProvider parameter, double-click to the right of the dataProvider heading in the Properties panel. A dialog box will open (see Figure 6.3), where you can add elements. Click on the + symbol to add an element.

> When you click the + symbol, a new element is created. The first element is named "label0" until you change the label. To do so, click on "label0" in the Value column and type in the text you would like the user to see for the first response option. You then change the data associated with this element by typing in the cell below. Then click the "+" symbol again to add the next element.

Figure 6.3.   Dialog box that opens when you click on dataProvider, where you can add elements to a List. Adobe product screenshot(s) reprinted with permission from Adobe Systems Incorporated.

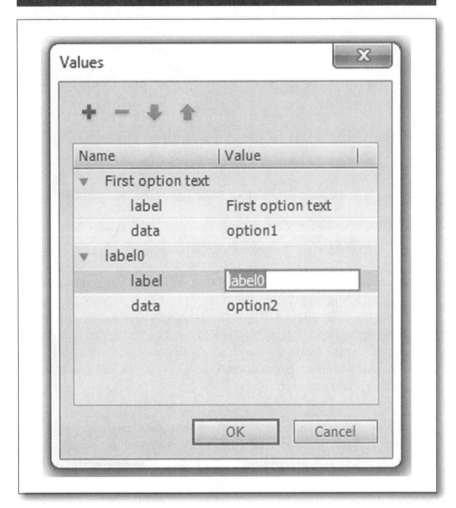

To continue with this example, add the following two elements to your List through the dataProvider parameter dialog box:

1) data = option1, label = This is the text of the first option

2) data = option2, label = This is the text of the second option

List elements can also be added in the code. This method is more versatile and you will need to use it if you ever want to add or replace elements while the program is active.

```
    /*To add an element to your List, reference the
List by its Instance Name, then use the addItem
method to define the label and data.*/

    lstResponses.addItem({label: "This is the text of
the third option", data: "option3"});
```

Note that both parentheses AND curly brackets need to be used. The curly brackets contain the definition of one element. The code shown earlier will add an element that will appear to the user as "This is the text of the third option" when the List is viewed, but it will store the value "option3" if you output the data parameter.

Sometimes it is also useful to remove or replace List items. Let us imagine we want to present a set of questions with different response options using the same Frame and List component. The questions can be presented one by one in a text field, and the answers will need to be loaded into the List component afresh for each question. To do this, we need to remove all of the current List elements after each question is answered, before adding a new set of elements.

```
    /*To remove all elements from a list, use the
removeAll method.*/

    lstResponses.removeAll();
```

After removing all the elements, you can add new elements with the `addItem` method. To see how the List scrolls, try adding more elements than would fit in your List.

Example: Making a Button Visible When the User Selects a Response From the List

In this example, we will make a previously invisible Button visible when the user selects an option from the List. To follow along with this example, you should already have a List called "lstResponses" on your Stage from the previous example, with a few possible response options. You will also need to do the following:

1) Add a Dynamic Text field to your Stage and give it the Instance Name "txtQuestion."

2) Type an appropriate question in "txtQuestion."

3) Add a Button to your Stage.

4) Give your Button the Instance Name "btnContinue" and the label "Continue."

5) Make the Button "btnContinue" invisible by clicking on Properties and unchecking the box next to visible.

6) Write an event listener that listens for a mouse click on the Button "btnContinue" and triggers a function called "continueClicked" (see Chapter 3: Navigation).

If you present the user with a question that requires a response, you do not want the user to be able to continue without first picking an element from the List. To achieve this, you can create a Button that does not become active until a List element is selected. In order to make a button active only once a List element is selected, you need to create an event that occurs upon selection of an element, and this event in turn will trigger the activation of the Button (see Figure 6.4).

First you need to add an event listener to the List that listens for an element in the List to be selected. Recall that previously we used an event listener to listen for a MouseEvent. In this case, we will be listening for an Event. In particular, Flash defines the selection of a List element as a CHANGE. When the event listener detects the selection of an element in the List, a function is executed to make a Button visible. Once this function has executed, the user will see the Button and can click it to continue. In the

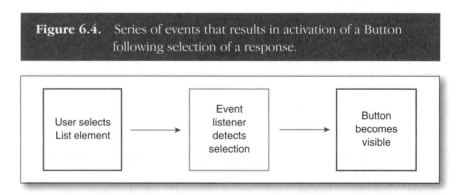

Figure 6.4. Series of events that results in activation of a Button following selection of a response.

following example, the Button will make the question and response options disappear. If you store your questions in an `Array` variable (see Chapter 5), you could use the Button to load the next question.

```
    /*Add an EventListener for your List, listening
for an event called Event.CHANGE.*/

    lstResponses.addEventListener(Event.CHANGE,
responseSelected);

    /*The   change   triggers   a   function   called
"responseSelected,"   which   makes   the   Button
"continueButton" visible.*/

    function responseSelected(evt:Event):void

    {

    btnContinue.visible = true;

    }

    /*This function makes the questions and response
options disappear when the Button is clicked.*/

    function continueClicked(evt:MouseEvent):void

    {

        txtQuestion.visible = false;

        lstReponses.visible = false;

    }
```

If your code is not working, double-check that you correctly named all your components and added the event listener to "btnContinue" as specified in the preliminary instructions. Just in case, what follows is all the code that should be in your Frame:

```
    stop();

    //Add  an  EventListener  to  a  Button  called
"btnContinue";
```
                                      Box (Continued)

Box (Continued)

```
    btnContinue.addEventListener(MouseEvent.CLICK,
continueClicked);

    //Add an EventListener to the List;

    lstResponses.addEventListener(Event.CHANGE,
responseSelected);

    /*This function makes the Button visible when
a List element is selected.*/

    function responseSelected(evt:Event):void

    {

        btnContinue.visible = true;

    }

    //This function makes the question and answers
invisible;

    function continueClicked(evt:MouseEvent):void

    {

        txtQuestion.visible = false;

        lstResponses.visible = false;

    }
```

Example: Activating a Visible Button When the User Selects a Response From the List

Instead of starting with an invisible Button and making it visible when the user selects a response from the list, you could start with an inactive Button. That is, the Button would not have an associated event listener, and you would add the event listener when a response from the List is selected. To make the following example work, use the program from the previous example and take these steps:

1) Set the Button "btnContinue" to visible.

2) Delete the event listener currently associated with "btnContinue."

3) Replace the function "responseSelected" with the following function:

```
    /*This function activates the Button when a
List element is selected.*/

    function responseSelected(evt:Event):void

    {

    /*Add an EventListener to a Button called
"btnContinue."*/

    btnContinue.addEventListener(MouseEvent.CLICK,
continueClicked);

    }
```

Example: Presenting a Warning Message if the User Tries to Continue Without Selecting a Response

Another option is to start with a Button that is already visible and enabled, but code different responses to the Button depending on whether a List element has been selected. For instance, you could add a warning if the Button is clicked without a List element being selected. To follow along with this example, use the project from the previous example and take the following steps:

1) Add a blank Dynamic Text field to your Stage and give it the Instance Name "txtWarning."

2) Clear all the code in your Frame except for the code for the function called "continueClicked" and the event listener that listens for the selection of a List element.

3) Add the following code to your Frame:

```
    /*Add an EventListener to the Button that will
trigger a warning.*/

    btnContinue.addEventListener(MouseEvent.CLICK,
clickWarning);

    /*This function makes a warning appear when the
Button is clicked.*/
```

Box (Continued)

```
Box  (Continued)

    function clickWarning(evt:MouseEvent):void

    {

        txtWarning.text = "Please select a response";

    }

    /*When a response from the List is selected,
this function removes the warning and changes the
function triggered by the Button click.*/

    function responseSelected(evt:Event):void

    {

    txtWarning.visible = false;

    btnContinue.removeEventListener(MouseEvent.
CLICK, clickWarning);

    btnContinue.addEventListener(MouseEvent.CLICK,
continueClicked);

    }
```

What have we done in this example? First, we put an event listener for the Button onto the Stage. This event listener calls a function that presents the warning message instead of allowing the user to continue. This is the default function attached to the Button. Now, when the user makes a selection, this event listener can be removed and replaced with an event listener that calls a different function.

Example: Storing the User's Selection From a List

Once the user selects a response, you will probably want to store it. You can store the data and/or label parameters of the selected List element in a variable. To do this, define a new String variable, just in case your data and/or label parameters contain nonnumerical symbols. Then pass to this variable the label or data parameter corresponding to the selected option once the user has made his or her selection. To be sure that the user has made his or her final selection when you pass those data to the variables, the code that passes the data should be within the function that is executed once the user submits his or her final response (i.e., in the "continueClicked" function in all of the previous examples). To follow along with this example, use any of the previous examples and delete your "continueClicked" function.

```
/*Define variables to store the label and data
parameters of the chosen response.*/

var responseLabel:String = new String;

var responseData:String = new String;

/*This function passes the label and data
parameters of the chosen response to the appropriate
variables.*/

function continueClicked(evt:MouseEvent):void

{

responseLabel=lstResponses.selectedItem.label;

responseData=lstResponses.selectedItem.data;

/*Check whether the parameters have been passed
to the variables.*/

trace(responseLabel);

trace(responseData);

}
```

2. The RadioButton Component

As demonstrated in the flowchart (Figure 6.1), the RadioButton component is most useful when there are a limited number of options for the user to choose from. The advantage of the RadioButton component over the List component is that all the options are visible on the Stage without the user having to scroll through a list. Instances of the RadioButton component can also be positioned in any kind of arrangement on the Frame, for example, in a horizontal row, so they are useful when you want the user to select a response on a scale. In this example, we use the RadioButton component to create a response scale consisting of five options.

> To add RadioButtons to a Frame, drag the RadioButton component onto the Stage from the Components panel. This creates one RadioButton. To create a scale with five options, drag five instances of the RadioButton component onto your Stage. To arrange the RadioButtons neatly on the Frame, you can use the tools in the Align panel (*Window → Align* or *Ctrl+K*).

Each instance of the RadioButton component that you place on your Stage needs to be given its own Instance Name. If you want to group multiple RadioButton instances into a group of response options, you can give them the same name with a different number suffix, that is, "rdb1," "rdb2," and so forth. In addition, you need to tell Flash to group the buttons together so that only one button in the group can be selected at any one time. To do this, you need to access the Component Parameters in the Properties panel. The following parameters can be edited:

`enabled` determines whether the RadioButton component can be accessed by the user (see notes for the List component).

`groupName` is used to group a set of response options for one question. Make sure the groupName is the same for all the buttons that form one set of response options.

`label` is what appears on the screen next to the RadioButton. Instead of setting this parameter, you can add text fields to your Stage to use as labels. This allows more flexibility in the positioning of your labels.

`labelPlacement` determines where you want the label to appear with respect to the RadioButton—the options are left, right, top, and bottom—but separate text fields still give you more flexibility.

`selected` determines whether that particular RadioButton is selected when it first appears on the screen. This parameter should be set to "false" for all the RadioButtons in your group so that none of the RadioButtons are selected when they first appear.

`value` is the data you can store if the user selects this RadioButton. This can be the same as or different than the label.

`visible` determines whether the RadioButton appears visible to the user when the Frame loads, and it is the same as for the List component.

Example: Storing RadioButton Responses

To follow along with this example, start a new project and do the following:

1) Drag five instances of the RadioButton component onto your Stage.

2) Give the five RadioButtons the Instance Names "rdb1" through "rdb5."

3) Give the five RadioButtons the values 1 through 5.

4) Add a Button to your Stage and give it the Instance Name "btnContinue."

As for the List component, you may only want to allow the user to continue once he or she has selected a RadioButton. Again, as for the List component, you could activate a Button when one of the RadioButtons is selected. Even though the RadioButtons are grouped, each RadioButton needs its own event listener. For the RadioButton component, the event that is being listened for is a MouseEvent, because Flash is listening out for the RadioButton to be clicked.

```
/*Each RadioButton needs its own EventListener,
but they can all call the same function.*/

    rdb1.addEventListener(MouseEvent.CLICK,
responseSelected);

    rdb2.addEventListener(MouseEvent.CLICK,
responseSelected);

    rdb3.addEventListener(MouseEvent.CLICK,
responseSelected);

    rdb4.addEventListener(MouseEvent.CLICK,
responseSelected);

    rdb5.addEventListener(MouseEvent.CLICK,
responseSelected);

    /*Since the Event registered by the RadioButtons
is a MouseClick, the associated function must have
a MouseEvent input.*/

    function responseSelected(evt:MouseEvent):void

    {

    /*Add an EventListener to a Button called
"btnContinue."*/

    btnContinue.addEventListener(MouseEvent.CLICK,
continueClicked);

    }
```

Once the response is selected and the Button is activated, allowing the user to continue, you need to store the user's response. To do this, you can pass the value parameter of the selected RadioButton to a String variable.

```
/*Create a variable to store the value of the
selected RadioButton.*/

var selectedRadioButton:String = new String;

function continueClicked(evt:MouseEvent):void

{

/*Reference any RadioButton in a group to
obtain data from the selected RadioButton.*/

selectedRadioButton =

String(rb1.group.selectedData);

trace(selectedRadioButton);

}
```

The statement in the "continueClicked" function essentially says this: Take the value of the selected RadioButton from the group that the rb1 RadioButton belongs to, turn it into a String, and pass it to the variable "selectedRadioButton." Here is an explanation of each of the parameters and methods in the statement:

`String()` translates the value in parentheses into a `String`. This ensures that you do not have any variable type incompatibilities when you pass data from the selected RadioButton to the variable you created to store that information.

"rb1" is the Instance Name of a RadioButton in your group.

`.group` references the group that the RadioButton "rb1" belongs to.

`.selectedData` references the value parameter of the selected RadioButton.

Example: Resetting the RadioButton Selection

If you would like to reuse the same Frame and RadioButton setup for multiple questions, you need to reset the selection so that none of the RadioButtons appear selected when the next question is loaded. You would think that this would be as simple as using the `.selected` parameter (i.e., `rb1.selected = false`, etc.), but unfortunately, once a RadioButton in a group has been selected, Flash requires that one RadioButton in the group (not necessarily the same one) remain selected. This is a glitch in Flash that many people have complained about.

In order to make the RadioButtons appear deselected, we can use a workaround, which involves adding another invisible RadioButton to the group and selecting this RadioButton after a response is made. To do this, use the program from the previous example and follow these steps:

1) Drag another instance of the RadioButton component onto your Stage and place it far away from the other, visible, RadioButtons (e.g., in a corner of the Frame).

2) Give this RadioButton the Instance Name "rdbInvisible."

3) In the Component Inspector, give this RadioButton the same `groupName` parameter as all the visible RadioButtons ("rdbGroup").

4) Uncheck the box by the visible parameter.

5) Add the following code to the function "continueClicked," after the response from the selected RadioButton has been stored:

```
/*This selects the invisible RadioButton thus
clearing the selection from the visible RadioButtons.*/

invisibleButton.selected = true;
```

Now, every time a response is made and the next question is loaded, the invisible RadioButton will be selected so that all the visible RadioButtons appear deselected and the user has to make a new response to continue. Do not add an event listener to this invisible RadioButton, otherwise the user will be able to continue without actually selecting a response.

3. CheckBox Component

Sometimes, you might want to ask the user a question that can have multiple answers. How could you do this using the components you are already familiar with? You could use the RadioButton component, but without grouping the RadioButtons, so that more than one can be selected at the same time. However, then you run into the problem that once a RadioButton has been selected, there is no way for the user to deselect it, because deselection of one RadioButton requires selection of another in the same group. So, the RadioButton component will not work when you want to allow multiple answers to one question.

How about the List component? This component has the property `allowMultipleSelection`, which if set to "true" allows more than one response to be selected by holding down CTRL. This works but can be quite cumbersome and nonintuitive for the user, although it may be a good option if you have a really long set of responses which would not all fit on one screen at the same time.

If your set of responses is not too long, though, the most convenient way to set up a question with multiple response functionality is to use the Check-Box component. With this component, users can check and uncheck as many answers as necessary and change their minds multiple times before submitting their final selection.

> To add check boxes to your Frame, drag an instance of the CheckBox component from the Components panel onto the Stage. This creates one CheckBox with an associated label, very similar to a RadioButton. To distinguish between Radio-Button and CheckBox components on your Stage, note that they are represented with a circle and square, respectively, as in the screenshot in Figure 6.5.

As with RadioButtons, each CheckBox will need to be given its own Instance Name. Unlike RadioButtons, however, CheckBoxes are not grouped together. For the CheckBox component, the following parameters can be set: `enabled`, `label`, `labelPlacement`, `selected`, and `visible`. These properties have been covered in the description of the List and/or RadioButton components.

If you want to make an event happen when a CheckBox is selected, you will follow the same procedure as for the RadioButton component. To make

Figure 6.5.   RadioButton and CheckBox components as they appear on the Stage in an uncompiled program. Adobe product screenshot(s) reprinted with permission from Adobe Systems Incorporated.

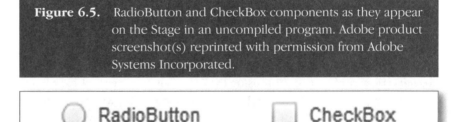

a function execute as soon as any one CheckBox is selected, each CheckBox will need its own event listener that listens for a `MouseEvent` (as for the RadioButton component).

To store responses associated with the selected CheckBoxes, you need to use an `Array`, because there can be more than one response. In order to store each response, you need to write separate conditional statements to determine whether each CheckBox has been selected.

Example: Storing Multiple Responses From the CheckBox Component in an Array

To follow along with this example, you need to create a new project and take the following steps:

1) Add three instances of the CheckBox component to your Stage.

2) Give them the Instance Names "chb1" through "chb3."

3) Give each CheckBox a unique label.

4) Add a Button to your Stage and give it the Instance Name "btnContinue."

5) Put an event listener in the code that listens for a mouse click on this Button and calls a function called "continueClicked."

6) Define a new `Array` called "selectedResponses."

```
    /*The following code determines whether each of
the CheckBoxes is selected and adds the relevant
CheckBox's label to the selectedResponses Array if a
CheckBox is selected.*/

    function continueClicked(evt:MouseEvent):void

    {

    /*For each CheckBox, determine whether it has
been selected;

    If the CheckBox has been selected, add its
label to the Array of selected responses.*/

                                Box (Continued)
```

```
Box (Continued)
    if(Response1.selected) selectedResponses.push
(Response1.label);

    if(Response2.selected) selectedResponses.push
(Response2.label);

    if(Response3.selected) selectedResponses.push
(Response3.label);

    trace(selectedResponses);

    //Clear the selection;

    chb1.selected = false;

    chb2.selected = false;

    chb3.selected = false;

}
```

Note that each of the conditionals is a separate `if` statement, rather than statements connected with `else if`. This is because you want each subsequent statement to be executed regardless of whether the previous condition was satisfied.

 ## 4. Slider Component

The Slider component is a useful tool for when you want to allow the user to make ratings on a continuous scale, for instance to indicate confidence. To add a Slider to your Frame, drag an instance of the Slider component from the Components panel onto the Stage.

You can set the following properties for the Slider:

`direction` can be set to horizontal or vertical and determines whether the Slider can be dragged up and down or left to right.

`enabled` and `visible` have the same settings as for previous components.

`liveDragging` determines whether Flash constantly registers an event while the user is dragging the Slider or only once the user lets go.

`minimum` and `maximum` determine the values at each end of the scale on the Slider.

snapInterval determines the interval to which the Slider snaps when it is moved. For instance, if you set this to 5 on a Slider with a 0–100 range, the user has to indicate his or her response rounded to the nearest multiple of 5. Set this to 0 to enable continuous ratings.

tickInterval determines the interval at which the ticks are placed next to the Slider as a reference point to the user.

value indicates the initial value that the Slider is set at when the Frame loads.

Example: Updating a Text Field as the User Drags a Slider

In this example, we create a Slider with a live update, allowing users to see what value they are currently selecting as they drag the Slider. To follow along with this example, start a new project and take the following steps:

1) Drag an instance of the Slider component to your Stage and give it the Instance Name "sldExample."

2) Enable the liveDragging property.

3) Add a Dynamic Text field to your Stage and give it the Instance Name "txtSliderValue."

4) Define a new String variable called "sliderValue."

5) Add the following code to your Frame:

```
    /*Add an EventListener to the Slider to register
a change.*/

    sldExample.addEventListener(SliderEvent.
CHANGE, updateSliderValue);

    /*This function is executed when there is a change
in the Slider.*/

    function updateSliderValue(evt:SliderEvent):void

    {

        /*Pass the current value of the Slider to
a String variable.*/
                                    Box (Continued)
```

```
Box (Continued)
      sliderValue = String(sldExample.value);

      /*Assign the contents of the String variable
to the text field.*/

      txtSliderValue.text = sliderValue;

  }
```

When you compile the program and drag the Slider, the value of the Slider should update dynamically in the text field.

Exercise: Try to write the following program using first the List component, then the RadioButton component, and last the CheckBox component for response selection:

Create a multiple-choice quiz with at least 10 questions and at least 4 options per question. Each question should have different answer options. Questions and answer options should be loaded from arrays. Response(s) to each question should also be stored in an array. After each response is made, ask the user to indicate his or her confidence on a Slider.

In this chapter, you learned that there are three components you might use to present questions along with response options for the user to pick from: the List component, the RadioButton component, and the CheckBox component. You learned that the RadioButton component is best used when there are few response options to pick from and only one response is allowed per question. If there are many response options to pick from but still only one response allowed, the List component is a better choice. Finally, if many responses per question can be picked at once, the CheckBox is the best choice. You learned how to set the properties for these components and populate them with questions and answers, both from menus and directly from the code.

Next, you learned how to determine which response was picked and store this information in a variable. The procedure differs somewhat from component to component. For the CheckBox component, you learned that the best way to store multiple responses to one question is in an `Array` variable.

You also learned that there are various ways to prevent the user from continuing without selecting a response: either you can make the continue button invisible unless a response is chosen, or you can leave it visible but deactivate it until a response is chosen, or you can present the user with a warning message if he or she tries to continue without first selecting a response. Finally, you learned about another component: the Slider. This component is useful for allowing participants to respond on a continuous scale, for instance to indicate their confidence in a response.

This chapter contained everything you need to know about programming questionnaires and surveys in Flash. With the tools included herein, there is no reason to use paper and pencil surveys in order to collect data from individuals. Rather, use CheckBoxes, RadioButtons, and Sliders to collect all that information. There is survey software available on the Internet which purports to do these things hassle free; in our experience, however, these tools often come with their own disadvantages. The programming basics that you have learned so far give you total control over the presentation and user experience of your surveys and experiments.

Resources

The following links are hot-linked for your convenience at http://www.sagepub.com/weinstein.

http://www.useit.com/alertbox/20040927.html
   A thorough discussion on when to use CheckBoxes versus RadioButtons.

http://www.actionscript.org/forums/showthread.php3?t=191468
   A discussion thread about deselecting RadioButtons.

http://www.adobe.com/devnet/flash/components.html
   An exhaustive list of the component reference pages provided by Adobe.

http://www.flashcomponents.net/component/slider_component.html
   Two implementations of the Slider component.

CHAPTER 7

CONDITION ASSIGNMENT
AND RANDOMIZATION

IN THIS CHAPTER, YOU WILL LEARN

- How to assign conditions by experimenter input or random selection
- How to generate a random number in a specified range
- How to use random numbers to randomize stimuli
- How to sample randomly from an array, with or without replacement
- How to randomize an entire array using a for loop

1. Manual Condition Assignment
Versus Randomization

In psychology experiments, and in most surveys, participants are often assigned to different conditions. You can either set up the program so that the experimenter can pick which condition to run for each user, or you can write code that will assign conditions automatically but randomly. In the first case, the experimenter will manually select the required condition for each participant. This technique is most useful when the experimenter wants maximum control over condition assignment, for instance, in order to ensure that the same number of participants are assigned to each condition. Randomization, on the other hand, can be useful if you are running an experiment or survey online. In this case, you might need to randomize condition assignment within the program, so that roughly the same number of people are randomly chosen to complete each condition. The advantage of this technique is that the program will automatically choose a condition without any user input. The disadvantage is that there is no way to determine the exact number of times each condition will be picked.

Condition assignment with experimenter input is very simple and only requires you to know how to recognize text input and write conditional statements. Although you already know both of these techniques, we put them together here to demonstrate how to allow condition selection.

Randomization is a little less straightforward, but it is easy enough to achieve once you learn how to generate random numbers that can then be used to determine which one of a set of actions is carried out. In this chapter, you will learn how to generate a random number in a given range and perform a different action for each different random number that can be generated. Loading the program will automatically execute the code for randomly picking a number. Depending on which random number is picked, a different action will be carried out.

2. Condition Selection With Experimenter Input

There are a few different ways you could implement counterbalancing with experimenter input. The simplest way, if there are only a few conditions, might be to add separate Buttons representing each condition to the first Frame of your Stage and have each Button call a different function that sets up the details of each condition. The Frame would look like the screenshot in Figure 7.1.

Example: Experimenter Presses a Different Button for Each Condition

To follow along with this example, create a Frame that looks like the screenshot in Figure 7.1, and give the three Buttons the Instance Names "btnCondition1" through "btnCondition3." You now need to write separate event listeners for each Button so that a different function is triggered when each of the conditions is selected.

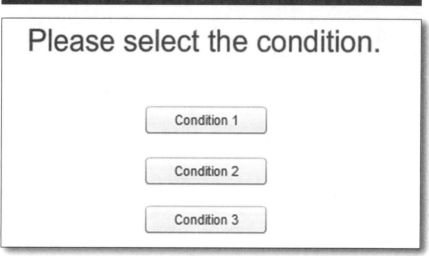

Figure 7.1. A simple way to allow the experimenter to select different versions of the program. Adobe product screenshot(s) reprinted with permission from Adobe Systems Incorporated.

```
    /*A click on each of the three Buttons triggers
a different function.*/

    btnCondition1.addEventListener(MouseEvent.
CLICK, setUpCondition1);

    btnCondition2.addEventListener(MouseEvent.
CLICK, setUpCondition2);

    btnCondition3.addEventListener(MouseEvent.
CLICK, setUpCondition3);
```

You also need to write separate functions for each condition to set up the details of that condition. It would also be a good idea to save the condition number in a variable.

```
    var conditionNumber:int = new int;

    function setUpCondition1(evt:MouseEvent):void

    {
```

```
        conditionNumber = 1;

        /*Here you would put all the actions asso-
ciated with this condition. For instance, you might
want to present a certain set of stimuli.*/

    }

    function setUpCondition2(evt:MouseEvent):void

    {

        conditionNumber = 2;

    }

    function setUpCondition3(evt:MouseEvent):void

    {

        conditionNumber = 3;

    }
```

Although the code described earlier is the easiest to grasp conceptually, it is also very inelegant. A more elegant code would combine all the conditions into one function and use conditional statements to determine the appropriate action based on which condition was selected.

Example: Experimenter Types in the Condition Number

One way to implement a conditional statement is to allow the user to type in the condition number and transfer this input to the "conditionNumber" variable. Then the conditional statement will check the value of "condition-Number" and proceed accordingly.

To follow along with this example, start a new project and do the following:

1) Add an Input Text field to your Stage and call it "txtCondition."

2) Add a Button to your Stage and call it "btnEnter."

3) Define a new int variable and call it "conditionNumber."

4) Add an event listener to your Stage that listens for a mouse click on "btnEnter" and calls the function "conditionSelected."

5) Set the `maxChars` property of "txtCondition" to 1.

6) Add a line of code that restricts input in "txtCondition" to the numerical characters 1, 2, and 3 only (see Chapter 4 for details on how to do that).

The "conditionSelected" function captures the user input from a text field and performs a different set of actions depending on which number the user typed. The following code assumes that only conditions 1–3 are valid.

```
function conditionSelected(evt:MouseEvent):void

{

conditionNumber = String(txtCondition.text);

trace("the condition picked is #", condition
Number);

if(conditionNumber == "1"){/*Here you would put
all the actions associated with condition 1.*/}

else if(conditionNumber == "2"){}

else if(conditionNumber == "3"){}

else{trace(conditionNumber, "is not a valid
condition number")}

}
```

You can also use similar logic to allow the experimenter to select the condition with radio buttons, which were covered earlier in the book (see Chapter 6).

Another useful way to select a condition is by assigning different conditions to different subject numbers. For instance, if you have two conditions, odd numbers are automatically assigned to condition A, and even numbers are automatically assigned to condition B. The experimenter inputs the subject number, and the code runs through a conditional statement to assign the appropriate condition based on this number. For this type of conditional statement where there are multiple conditions (i.e., if the number is 1, or 3, or 5, or 7 versus 2, or 4, or 6, or 8, etc.), you are better off using the `switch` method rather than `if` statements. You can learn more about this by checking out the websites listed in the Resources section.

3. Randomization: Picking a Condition Without Experimenter Input

The easiest way to pick a random condition is to have Flash generate a random number and use this number to determine which condition is selected. Unfortunately, though, there is no method in Flash for generating a random integer, so we need to complete a few additional steps. What Flash can do is generate a random number between 0 and 1; we can then transform this into a random integer.

Example: Selecting a Condition Based on a Randomly Generated Number

For this example, simply start a new blank project. All the work is in the code. First, we need to create a variable that can handle decimal places to store the random number Flash generates. The `int` variable will not work here because it only stores whole numbers, so we use the `Number` variable (see Chapter 2 for details on the different data types). Next, we need to get Flash to generate a random number. We do this by using the `Math.random` method, which produces a random number between 0 and 1.

```
var randomNumber:Number = new Number;

/*To generate a random number, call the Math.
random method.*/

randomNumber = Math.random();
```

Remember, a statement such as this one changes the contents of the variable on the left-hand side of the equation to the value on the right-hand side of the equation. The method `Math.random` ends with an empty set of parentheses because you are not telling this command to perform an action on any piece of information. If you put the code in the Frame (rather than within any specific function), the program will generate a new random number every time it is compiled. Remember to `trace` the contents of "randomNumber" to check that the random number generation is working.

Now let us imagine that you want to pick one of three conditions (numbered 1, 2, and 3). In order for the random number generated by Flash to be of any use to us, we need some way of converting it into one of these integers. One way to do so is to place the random number produced into one of three bins:

Bin #1:	0	< randomNumber <	0.33
Bin #2:	0.33	< randomNumber <	0.66
Bin #3:	0.66	< randomNumber <	1

This will result in, on average, an equal number of assignments to each of the three bins. Each of these three bins could represent a condition. One way of telling the program to assign the random numbers to bins would be to write a conditional statement to create these bins (i.e., if the number is smaller than 0.33, then the condition is equal to 1, etc.), but there is actually an easier way. We simply need to multiply the randomly generated number by the number of conditions (in this case, 3) and round up the resulting number. This will give us an equal chance of getting each of the numbers in the specified range. If this does not seem intuitive, try the calculation out on the following numbers: 0.2324, 0.5867, 0.9234. Using the operations described, you should end up with 1, 2, and 3, respectively.

```
//Multiply the random number by 3;

randomNumber = randomNumber*3;
```

As you can see if you `trace` the variable "randomNumber" after the calculation, at the moment, your random number is not rounded. To turn your number into a 1, a 2, or a 3, you need to round up the random number after multiplying it by 3. To round up numbers, you can use one of the following three methods. In each case, put the value you want to round in parentheses after calling your method of choice. The value in parentheses could be an actual number or a variable name.

1) `Math.ceil` to round up—when the smallest value you want to pick is 1

2) `Math.floor` to round down—when the smallest value you want to pick is 0

3) `Math.round` to round to the nearest integer (up or down)

In this case, we use `Math.ceil` because the smallest number we want to be able to pick is 1.

```
//Round up the random number;

randomNumber = Math.ceil(randomNumber);
```

Using this code, the program should now successfully pick a random number from 1 to 3. Every time you compile the program, a new integer will be picked randomly from 1, 2, or 3. You can summarize the three steps (random number generation, multiplication by 3, and rounding up) into one equation to produce a succinct single line of code:

```
/*Generate a random number, multiply it by 3, and
round it up.*/

randomNumber = Math.ceil(Math.random()*3);
```

You can use this equation to generate a random integer from any range of integers. To change the number of different conditions (integers) you are picking from, simply multiply the random number you generate by the number of different conditions you would like the program to pick from (in our example, we use 3). To offset the numbers (i.e., if you want to pick from 3–5 instead of 1–3), add the number by which you want to offset (relative to 1) to the rounded number. Here is the general formula for any number of conditions and any offset:

```
/*randomNumber = <offset number> + Math.ceil(Math.
random() * <number of conditions>)

   Example: Formula for picking a condition from
11 through 15*/

randomNumber = 10 + Math.ceil(Math.random()*5);
```

As with the experimenter-selected condition assignment in the first section, we want the program to execute different actions depending on which condition is picked. As in that example, we can use a conditional statement to carry out a different action for each condition number.

4. Using Random Number Generation to Randomize Stimuli

Now let us imagine that you want to present elements that are stored in an array in a random order. There are a few different ways you could achieve this. One way is to generate a random number on each trial with the total number of trials as the upper bound. The random number generated on each trial is then used to determine which elements from the array are displayed by selecting the element whose index matches the random number.

Example: Sampling Randomly From an Array With Replacement

To follow along with this example, you will need to start a new project and do the following:

1) Define an `int` variable called "randomNumber."

2) Create an `Array` called "originalArray" and populate it with a few elements.

3) Add a Button to your Stage and give it the Instance Name "btnRandomElement."

4) Add an event listener that listens for a mouse click on "btnRandomElement" and calls the function "newRandomElement."

```
    /*The following function will trace a random
element from the array "originalArray" each time it
executes.*/

    function newRandomElement(evt:MouseEvent):void

        {

        /*Select a random number no higher than the
length of the array.*/

        randomNumber  =  Math.floor(Math.random()
*originalArray.length);

        trace(originalArray[randomNumber]);

        }
```

Note that we used `Math.floor` here instead of `Math.ceil` because our array has an element in index 0. If you follow these directions, you will be sampling from the array with replacement—that is, some items may be selected more than once. If you only want to select each item once, you will have to include another step in your code to make sure that no item is picked more than once.

Example: Sampling Randomly From an Array Without Replacement

One way of sampling without replacement is to substitute the element at each sampled index with blank text (`null`). You then tell the program to keep picking a new random number until it finds the index of an element that has not been used (i.e., the contents of which are not blank text). Another thing you have to do if you want to sample without replacement is include a counter so that you can stop the function from executing when all the items in the array have been exhausted.

To follow along with this example, use your project from the previous example and define an `int` variable called "i" to be your counter. Delete your "newRandomElement" function and replace it with the one that follows.

```
function newRandomElement(evt:MouseEvent):void

  {

  /*Stop picking new elements when the counter
exceeds the length of the array.*/

        if(i == originalArray.length)

        {

                trace("end of array reached");

        }

        else

        {

        //Pick the first random number;
                                        Box (Continued)
```

```
Box (Continued)
            randomNumber =

            Math.floor(Math.random()*originalArray
.length);

    /*Keep picking a random number until an unused
element is found.*/
        while (originalArray[randomNumber] == null)

            {

            randomNumber =

            Math.floor(Math.random()*original
Array.length);

            }

        trace(originalArray[randomNumber]);
    //Remove the element from the original array;
        originalArray[randomNumber] = null;
    //Update the counter;
        i++;

        }

    }
```

This function first checks whether all the elements in the array have been exhausted. If not, it finds a random element from the array "originalArray" that has not been selected by checking whether the element at the randomly generated index has any content. If the element at that index is blank, a new random number is generated. At the end of the function, the element that has just been traced is replaced with blank text and the counter is updated.

Example: Randomizing an Entire Array

Another, perhaps easier way of presenting items from an array in a random order is to randomize the whole array and then work through the newly randomized array sequentially. You essentially do the same thing described earlier (picking a new random number and selecting the element associated with its index in the array) over and over until you have a new array full of the items in your original array but arranged in random order. The benefit of this technique is that you get the randomization out of the way in one go. You can either type this code straight into your Frame so that it executes when the Frame loads or in a function that is only called when you enter the Frame for the first time. This is important if you are going to return to that Frame later but want to maintain the same order.

To follow along with this example, you can use your project from the previous example, but you also need to create a new array called "randomizedArray." Leave this array blank for now—it will store the elements in your original array in a random order. Put the following code anywhere in your Frame so that it runs when the Frame loads.

```
    /*Start this loop at 0; end it when the end of the
array is reached; add 1 to the counter on each loop.*/

    for (i = 0; i < originalArray.length; i++)

    {

    //Pick a random number;

    randomNumber =Math.floor (Math.random ()*original
Array.length);

    /*Keep picking a random number until an unused
element is found*/

    while (originalArray[randomNumber] == null)

        {

        randomNumber =

    Math.floor (Math.random ()*originalArray.
length);

        }

        //Add the selected element to the new array;

        randomizedArray.push (originalArray[random
Number]);

        //Remove the element from the original array;

        originalArray[randomNumber] = null;

    }
```

The `for` loop will be executed the number of times that is equivalent to the number of elements in your original array. Each time the loop executes, a new random element is selected from "originalArray" and pushed into "randomizedArray" so that the elements in that array are now in a random order. Note that after execution of this `for` loop, "originalArray" is now entirely composed of blank elements (see Figure 7.2).

Exercise: Write a program that will select a random participant number from 1–50 and randomly assign each new participant to one of two different order conditions. Participants in condition 1 will see a list of words in the order they appear in an array. Participants in condition 2 will see the same list of words but in a random order.

In this chapter, you learned how to assign the user to a different condition, either by allowing the experimenter to choose the condition or letting the program choose a condition at random. When allowing the experimenter to choose the condition, you could either set it up so that the experimenter has to click on a different button to select each condition, or you could let the experimenter enter a condition number. In order to make the program select a condition at random, you learned how to generate a random number and translate it into an integer in a specified range.

Delving deeper into randomization, you learned how to use randomly generated numbers to randomize presentation order of stimuli, questions, or sections in your program. You learned how to sample from an array with replacement (an item could be shown more than once) or without

Figure 7.2. Array contents before and after randomization.

0	1	2	3	4	5	index
Dog	Cat	Lion	Tiger	Mouse	Rat	originalArray
null	null	null	null	null	null	randomizedArray

0	1	2	3	4	5	index
null	null	null	null	null	null	originalArray
Cat	Tiger	Dog	Lion	Rat	Mouse	randomizedArray

replacement (each item would only be shown once). Randomization is fundamental to good experimental design. This chapter taught you the skills you need to both (1) randomly sample and (2) randomly assign to experimental conditions—things that may be essential for even the most basic surveys and experiments.

Resources

The following links are hot-linked for your convenience at http://www .sagepub.com/weinstein.

http://actionsnippet.com/?p=1640
  A trick for making your randomly generated numbers more variable.

http://digitalmedia.oreilly.com/helpcenter/actionscript30cookbook/chapter1
  .html?page=6
  Sample chapter from the ActionScript 3.0 Cookbook, explaining the switch statement.

http://as3-blog.net/?p=578
  An advanced look at shuffling around the contents of an array.

http://snipplr.com/view/11307/as3-randomize-array/
  Another method of randomizing the contents of an array.

CHAPTER **8**

USING TIMERS AND RECORDING REACTION TIME

IN THIS CHAPTER, YOU WILL LEARN

- How to create a date/time stamp
- Two methods of controlling time—an easy method and a better method
- How to create a countdown timer
- How to record timings (e.g., reaction times in an experiment or the time it took the user to answer a question in your survey)
- About the accuracy and limitations of Flash for timings

Flash is capable of controlling and recording time, which is important for surveys and experiments. In this chapter, we will show you how to output the date and time when users access your survey or experiment, make events last for specific durations (e.g., present a word for 3 seconds), create countdown timers, and record the time it takes the user to make responses.

1. Date and Time Stamps

Date and/or time stamps are very useful and especially helpful if you are running your survey or experiment online. With a date and time stamp when the program first loads and another when the user responds to the last question, you can figure out how quickly you are getting respondents and how long they are taking to complete your program. To return the current time stamp, define a new Date variable without passing any parameters to it.

```
//Return the current full date, time, and time zone;
var datePlayed = new Date();
```

The output you would get if you subsequently traced the "datePlayed" variable would look something like this:

Fri Mar 19 10:13:49 GMT-0500 2010

If you want to return more than one date/time stamp in your program, simply define a new Date variable each time.

Example: Accessing Individual Properties of a Date and Time Stamp

You can also use individual values in the date stamp separately by calling the relevant property. In all of the following trace statements, the comment indicates what value would be sent to output if the date was Friday 03/19/2010.

```
//This would return "2010";
trace(datePlayed.fullYear);

/*Month is in a numeric format with 0 for
January up to 11 for December. The following trace
statement would return "2":*/
trace(datePlayed.month) ;

/*Date is the day of the month (1 to 31). The
following trace statement would return "19":*/
trace(datePlayed.date);

/*This is the day of the week as a number (0-7)
where 0 = Sunday. The following trace statement
would return a "5":*/
trace(datePlayed.day);
```

The other properties you can reference are hours, minutes, seconds, and milliseconds.

2. Experimenter Controlled Timings Using the setTimeout Method

Another important purpose of Flash's timing system is to enable you to set timings in your program. Let us say we want to present a list of 10 words, one at a time, for 3 seconds each. That is, we want each subsequent word to appear not because the user does something, but because the program is alerted that 3 seconds have passed. You already know that you need an array to store your stimuli. However, you cannot control the presentation of the words using what you have learned so far, because all of our functions were either called from the code when the Frame loaded or by a user-initiated event (such as a MouseEvent). There are many different ways to trigger functions based on elapsed time. Here we consider two methods: setTimeout and Timer. The former is easier to implement, but the latter is considered to be the best practice in ActionScript 3.0.

Example: Setting Timings With the setTimeout Method

The setTimeout method calls a function after a specified amount of time has elapsed. This method is useful if you want to use basic timings, such as forcing the user to stay on a Frame for a minimum amount of time before moving on.

To follow along with this example, take the following steps:

1)   Define an array called "wordList" and populate it with 10 elements.

2)   Define a counter called "i" and give it the initial value of 0.

3)   Add a Dynamic Text field to your Stage and give it the Instance Name "txtWord."

When you call the setTimeout method, you need to pass it through two properties:

1)   The function or method to execute when the time has elapsed

2)   The amount of time in milliseconds that you want the program to wait before executing the function or method

```
    /*Call the function "nextTrial" after 3 seconds
(3000 milliseconds) have elapsed.*/

    setTimeout(nextTrial, 3000);
```

Next, you have to figure out where to put this code. If you want to present a new word every 3 seconds, you could put the code within the function that loads the next trial so that it triggers itself after 3 seconds have passed. However, you also need to call this function once from within the code to start the first trial.

```
    //Start the first trial;

    nextTrial();

    function nextTrial():void

    {

    //Present the next word;

    txtWord.text = wordlist[i]

    /*If the end of the array has been reached,
call the "endList" function.*/

    if(i == (wordList.length-1)){setTimeout
(endList, 3000)};

    else

    {

    //Execute the next trial in 3 seconds;

    setTimeout(nextTrial, 3000);

    //Update the counter;

    i++;

    }

    }

    function endList():void

    {

        txtWord.text = "end of list";

    }
```

The function "nextTrial" first traces the next element in the array by referencing the element at the index of the counter. Then, if the counter is one less than the length of the array (one less because of the element in index 0), the setTimeout method is called to execute the function again after 3 seconds. Once the counter has reached 9 (i.e., all 10 words have been shown), the setTimeout method calls a different function to end the presentation.

As an aside, the function is a variant of what programmers call recursion, because the body of the function contains a call to the function itself. This technique, although occasionally complicated to implement, is sometimes necessary to construct optimal, elegant code.

Example: Using setTimeout to Set Off a Series of Events

You can also combine multiple calls to the setTimeout method to create a series of events; for instance, imagine you want to insert a 1-second pause between each of the words. You will be creating two functions—one that presents each word and another that adds a pause between words. The flowchart in Figure 8.1 summarizes the process.

Figure 8.1. Flowchart showing that the presentWord function triggers the presentPause function in 3 seconds, which in turn triggers the presentWord function in 1 second, until the end of the list is reached.

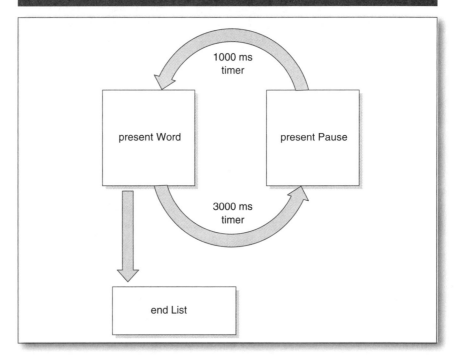

To follow along with this example, you can use the program from the previous example, but comment out the initial call to the "nextWord" function.

```
//Start the first trial;

presentWord();

function presentWord():void

{

    txtWord.text = wordList[i];

    if(i == (wordList.length-1)){setTimeout
(endList, 3000)};

else

{

//Present the word for 3 seconds;

setTimeout(presentPause, 3000);

i++;

}

}

function presentPause():void

{

    //Clear the text;

    txtWord.text = "";

    //Present the next word in 1 second;

    setTimeout(presentWord, 1000);

}
```

In some cases, you might need to cancel a setTimeout method. For instance, imagine you want to present each word for 3 seconds or until the user makes a response (whichever is the shorter duration). In this case, you interrupt or cancel the `setTimeout` call, so that you can move on to the next trial immediately rather than waiting for the full 3 seconds. If you do not cancel the `setTimeout` call, a new trial is triggered after 3 seconds even if the program has already initiated the next trial as a result of a user event. To be able to cancel a `setTimeout` method, you need to assign it to a variable when you define it.

Example: Overriding a setTimeout Call With User Input

To follow along with this example, use the setup from the first example in this chapter. Delete the "nextTrial" function you used for that example, and replace it with the one below. Remember to initially call the "nextTrial" function from the code.

1) This "nextTrial" function is essentially the same as that of the first example except for the following changes: An event listener has been added so that the end of a trial can be triggered by a keystroke.

2) The setTimeout method was assigned to a named variable "wordDuration" and this name was used to cancel the setTimeout call.

3) A new function "endTrial" was defined to clear the setTimeout call when the user hit a key.

```
    /*Define an integer variable that will later be
assigned the setTimeout method.*/

    var wordDuration = new int;

    //Add an EventListener to respond to a keystroke;

    stage.addEventListener(KeyboardEvent.KEY_DOWN,
endTrial);

    function nextTrial():void

    {

    txtWord.text = wordList[i];

    if(i == (wordList.length-1)){setTimeout
(endList, 3000)}

    else
```

```
    {

    /*Assign  the  setTimeout  call  to  the  variable
"wordDuration."*/

    wordDuration = setTimeout(nextTrial, 3000);

    i++;

    }

    }

    /*This  function  is  triggered  by  the  user
pressing a key*/

    function endTrial(KeyboardEvent):void

    {

    /*Clear the setTimeout call associated with the
variable "wordDuration."*/

    clearTimeout(wordDuration);

    trace("trial terminated by user");

    //Start the next trial;

    nextTrial();

    }
```

3. Experimenter Controlled Timings Using the Timer

The `Timer` is a little trickier than `setTimeout` but is recommended as a replacement for `setTimeout`, which may be phased out in later versions of ActionScript. The `Timer` allows you to trigger events when a specified delay has elapsed, and it also allows you to do this multiple times. To define a Timer, you need to give it three pieces of information:

1) A name

2) The amount of time in milliseconds that you want to pass before the Timer runs out

3) The number of times you would like the Timer to execute

```
    /*Basic syntax to declare and define a new
Timer (The bolded words will be replaced with the
relevant parameters.)*/

    var trialTimer:Timer=new Timer (<trialTimerDelay>,
  <trialTimerRepeatCount>);
```

<trialTimerDelay> will be replaced with the length of time in milliseconds before you want the Timer to go off.

<trialTimerRepeatCount> will be replaced with the number of times you want the Timer to loop.

The delay of the Timer is once again set in milliseconds. You also need to define the number of times you want the Timer to loop, which here could be the number of trials in your block plus one for the final screen. Note that if you use a Timer to present stimuli, the first word (and subsequent words) will be presented *after* the duration specified on the Timer has elapsed, rather than presenting the words *for* a specified amount of time.

Example: Setting Timings With a Timer

To follow along with this example, you can use any program from the previous examples but delete the initial call to your "nextTrial" function. We will write a different function, "nextTimerTrial," to present words.

```
    /*Define a new Timer variable with the delay
and count parameters.*/

    var trialTimer:Timer = new Timer(3000, 11);

    /*Add an EventListener that listens for the
Timer to run out.*/

    trialTimer.addEventListener(TimerEvent.TIMER,
nextTimerTrial);

    //Start the Timer;

    trialTimer.start();

    //This function is triggered by the Timer;
```

```
function nextTimerTrial(TimerEvent):void

{

    if(i == 10){endList()};

    else{txtWord.text = wordList[i], i++}

}
```

First, the Timer is defined and given a duration of 3 seconds and a count of 11. Next, an event listener is added so that every time the Timer goes off, the "nextTimerTrial" function is executed. The Timer is started from within the code. When 3 seconds have elapsed, "nextTimerTrial" executes. This function first checks to see if the end of the list has been reached and triggers the "endList" function if this is the case; otherwise, a new word is presented and the counter is updated, as in all the previous examples.

Instead of setting a finite number of counts, you can also use 0, which means that the Timer keeps running indefinitely, unless you tell it to stop, or 1, which means that the Timer will run only once, unless you tell it to start again. You can also stop the Timer by calling `trialTimer.stop()`, which is useful if you want to interrupt a trial due to user input. Finally, you can reset the Timer by calling `trialTimer.reset()`, which resets the count index (not the count limit) back to 0. This is useful if you want to present multiple blocks of stimuli using the same Timer. See the Resources section for links with more information on how to use these methods.

4. Countdown Timers

Now let's say you want to create a Timer which counts down until the end of a predetermined time period. You want to show a text field, which displays the countdown and then tells you that time is up.

Example: Counting Down the Seconds Using a Timer

To follow along with this example, create a new blank project and add a Dynamic Text field to your Stage; give it the Instance Name "txtCountdown."

To count down the seconds, you need to define a Timer with a delay of 1,000 milliseconds, and the number of counts will be the number of seconds you want in your countdown. You then need to create two event listeners: one for each time the Timer reaches the delay, as in the previous examples (`TimerEvent.TIMER`), and one for when the Timer completes (`TimerEvent.TIMER_COMPLETE`).

Every time the Timer reaches the specified delay, the program will display the number of seconds remaining before the Timer completes in a text field. To determine how many times the Timer has gone off, you can use the `.currentCount` property. You can then calculate the number of seconds remaining on the Timer by subtracting the number of times the Timer has gone off from the total number of counts you have set for the Timer.

```
/*Define a Timer variable with a delay of 1
second that will fire 60 times.*/

var countdownTimer:Timer = new Timer(1000, 60)

/*You need to call this function from the code
initially so that the time remaining displays
before the first second has elapsed.*/

nextTick(null);

//Start the Timer;

countdownTimer.start();

/*Add an EventListener that responds to the
Timer*/

countdownTimer.addEventListener(TimerEvent.
TIMER, nextTick)

function nextTick(TimerEvent):void

{

//Display the number of seconds remaining;

txtCountdown.text = String(60 - countdownTimer.
currentCount)

}

/*Add an EventListener that responds to completion
of the Timer.*/
```

```
countdownTimer.addEventListener(TimerEvent.
TIMER_COMPLETE, countdownFinished);

    function countdownFinished(TimerEvent):void

    {

    txtCountdown.text ="The countdown has finished."

    }
```

5. Recording Reaction Times

To record how long it takes the user to do something (commonly known as reaction time), you can use the `getTime` method. This method returns the number of milliseconds that have elapsed since midnight January 1, 1970, but what this effectively means is that you obtain a number in milliseconds that you can compare to another number once the time you want to measure has passed. The syntax is very simple: You use the `getTime` method when you want to start recording time and again when you stop; you then get the difference in time between those two points. So, to record reaction times, follow these steps:

2) Define a variable that will store the reaction time.

2) Start recording time by assigning the current time to this variable.

3) Stop recording time by subtracting the current time from the start time recorded in the variable.

```
    /*Define a variable that will store the reaction
time*/

    var elapsedTime:Number = new Number;

    /*Put this line whenever you want to start
recording time*/

                                    Box (Continued)
```

```
Box (Continued)

    elapsedTime = getTimer();

    /*Put this line whenever you want to stop
recording time*/

    elapsedTime = (getTimer() - elapsedTime);

    /*The variable "elapsedTime" now contains the
reaction time*/

    trace(elapsedTime);
```

 ## 6. Accuracy of Timings in Flash

A common concern with regard to running surveys and experiments online is that timings will not be as accurate as those collected in the lab using specialist software. This issue has been addressed thoroughly in a paper by Reimers and Stewart (Reimers, S., & Stewart, N. [2007]. Adobe Flash as a medium for online experimentation: A test of RT measurement capabilities. *Behavior Research Methods, 39,* 365–370), who have been using Flash to collect data on decision-making behavior. The gist of the paper is that the timings Flash reports when the program is run online are overestimates of those reported by more precise software developed specifically for recording reaction times. To be precise, the timings reported by Flash are roughly 30 milliseconds (or .03 of a second) longer than those reported by E-Prime and the like. However, this affects all timings equally and does not create any additional variability in the timings data. This means it is fine to use Flash for timings, but there is one important exception, detailed here.

The only thing Flash should not be used for is to present stimuli for extremely short durations (anything less than about 64 milliseconds). Here is why it is best not to use Flash to present stimuli for extremely short durations. (You can skip this section if you do not plan to use it in this manner.) When manipulating the visual display, you are limited by the framerate set within Flash and the refresh rate of your browser and/or monitor. The framerate, measured in frames per second (fps), determines how often the visual display can update with new content. The default framerate is 24 fps, which means that the screen should update every 41.666 milliseconds. This also interacts with the screen refresh rate of your monitor, which is typically 60 Hz (that is, it updates every 16.666 milliseconds). If you have a stimulus presented for "25 milliseconds" with a 24 fps framerate, in reality there will be a margin of error of up to 41.666 + 16.666 milliseconds (depending on when the code executes). Because this error is random noise, it does not matter if you are presenting stimuli for seconds at a time—this word of caution only relates to extremely precise timings.

Exercise 1: Create a game that requires the user to complete 10 math problems correctly to win. The user has 120 seconds total, and a new problem appears every 10 seconds. If a user's response to a problem is faster than 10 seconds, the next problem appears. A countdown Timer tells the user how many seconds are left in the game.

Exercise 2: Take the program you created in the exercise from "Chapter 6: Questionnaire Tools" and add a measure of response time for each question.

In this chapter, you learned how to use the tools Flash provides for manipulating and recording timings. The first thing you learned was how to create a date and time stamp to put in your data output. You learned that this is useful for figuring out whether the user spent a reasonable amount of time completing your experiment or survey and to determine how many responses you are getting per hour/day/week. You then learned about controlling timings in your program. You have a choice between the somewhat more intuitive "setTimeout" method and the more complex but also more flexible "Timer." Finally, you learned how to record the time it takes the user to do something by recording two points in time and finding the difference between the two. All of this information came with a caveat about the accuracy of timings in Flash—the take-home message is that accuracy is pretty good, unless you are interested in presenting things on the screen for less than about 100 milliseconds at a time.

The skills discussed in this chapter can be readily applied to many practical problems: limiting the amount of time an individual has to make a response, recording how long it takes for the user to make decisions, or keeping track of how long it takes someone to complete an experiment.

Resources

The following links are hot-linked for your convenience at http://www .sagepub.com/weinstein.

http://actionsnippet.com/?p=385
   How to use the date stamp to automatically generate a unique ID for each user.

http://www.adobe.com/designcenter/flash/articles/flacs3it_astimeline_print .html
   A basic overview of how to use the Timer class.

http://layersmagazine.com/build-a-simple-countdown-timer-in-flash.html
   Creating a countdown timer in Flash. Includes more advanced design techniques as well as code samples.

http://www.ucl.ac.uk/~ucjtsre/B210.pdf
   Academic journal article measuring the accuracy of reaction time measurement in Flash.

http://www.flashandmath.com/howtos/eztimer/index.html
   An advanced look at Timer performance, with a demonstration of the error margin.

CHAPTER 9

SAVING DATA

IN THIS CHAPTER, YOU WILL LEARN

- That there are two main alternatives for how you can output your data
- How to store multiple pieces of data in one String
- How to create a template for your data output
- How to test your output to make sure it fits the template

1. Data Output

So far, we have written programs that have been functional from the user's perspective but somewhat useless to us because they do not actually record any data that we can look at later. Whenever you have been sending information to the Output window using the `trace` method, this information is only available to be viewed via the Flash interface and is not accessible if you run the program outside of Flash (i.e., in a Flash player or on the Web). We need to use a different method to save data for output. We then need to send the data out of Flash and into a usable format that can later be accessed and used for analysis.

The most efficient way to output data is to create one `String` variable that will contain all of the data for one user. This is the most efficient method because if you are running the survey or experiment online, multiple users may be accessing your program at the same time. If all of one user's data is output on one line, this makes it easy to determine how many users have completed and ensures that you can easily determine where one user's information ends and another's begins. The `String` variable containing all of one user's data is then sent to a text file, where every row of data corresponds to one user.

Another alternative is to output data through String variables for each "observation" rather than for each user, for instance, sending information about each answered question as soon as it has been input, instead of all at one time, once the end of the program has been reached. This method has several advantages: (1) Some data will have still been collected and output even if the user quits the program early or the program malfunctions (as unlikely as that will be after reading this book!), (2) the resulting data layout may be easier for some sorts of analyses (e.g., item-by-item analyses), and (3) you can track where a subject is in the experiment by observing incoming observations on the server. However, this method does carry with it several disadvantages: (1) If several users are accessing the program at the same time, the data will not be organized by users; (2) if the program contains multiple phases or types of questions, the output might be harder to untangle; and (3) you may have to output data from different sections to different text files and create multiple templates (discussed later) for interpreting your data.

After obtaining a little bit of experience programming in Flash, you will have an improved sense of the best output method for your particular needs. This chapter discusses the first method of outputting data (i.e., outputting all of the information for one user once he or she reaches the end), but the principles can be applied easily to the second method (outputting information by question or section).

Example: Using a String Variable to Store Output

To create your output variable, first define a new `String` variable called "output." Then, whenever you get to any part of the program that produces data you want to save, you can add this data to the variable "output." First, though, you need to turn the data into a string, to ensure that there are no data type incompatibilities. After that, you append the latest piece of data to the variable "output" (this is also called *concatenating*). Each time you do this, the new data is added to whatever is already saved in the variable. For instance, imagine your program randomly picks a condition for each participant (numbered 1, 2, or 3) and stores it in a variable called "conditionNumber." You would like to output the chosen condition to your data file.

```
/*Append   the   contents   of   the   variable
"conditionNumber" to the variable "output."*/

output += String(conditionNumber);
```

Now, imagine you appended multiple pieces of data to this variable. You would get a nonsense string of numbers and letters, and it would be impossible to know where one data point ended and another began. To separate the data points in the variable from each other, you can insert a special character after each variable. Then, when you open up the text file that contains your data in a program such as Excel, you can use that special character to delimit (i.e., separate) the fields so that each data point is read into a different column. Asterisks are a good choice because they are very rarely (if ever) input by the typical user, so they are unlikely to interfere with your output. As a safety precaution, you could also exclude the asterisk from any Input Text field using the `restrict` method (see "Chapter 4: Working With Text and Keystrokes").

```
/*Append an asterisk to the output variable to
delineate one piece of information from the next.*/

output += "*";
```

In addition to sending the contents of individual variables to output (e.g., variables that store individual pieces of information such as age, gender, etc.), you may want to send the contents of an entire array to your output variable. This would be useful if, for instance, you used an array to save a set of responses to a series of questions. To send the contents of an array to your output variable in a readable format, you need to append an asterisk after each element in the array. If you add the whole array to your output variable without doing this, you would end up with one long string, without any delimitation between the elements in your array (see Figure 9.1).

To intersperse asterisks between each element in an array, you can send the array to a function that cycles through the array and adds each element followed by an asterisk to a new string. By setting up this function, you can then send as many arrays as you like to it and return strings of data points separated by asterisks that you can then append to your output variable.

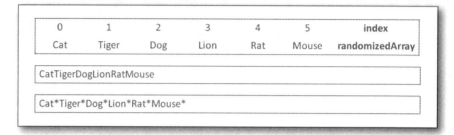

Figure 9.1. The contents of an array, output without delineation between elements, and output with asterisks between each element.

0	1	2	3	4	5	index
Cat	Tiger	Dog	Lion	Rat	Mouse	randomizedArray

CatTigerDogLionRatMouse

Cat*Tiger*Dog*Lion*Rat*Mouse*

To follow along with this example, take the following steps:

1) Define a `String` variable called "output." (You should already have this from the previous example.)

2) Define a new `Array` variable called "responseArray" and populate it with a few elements.

The following function takes an array and temporarily labels it as "inputArray." A new temporary `String` variable called "outputString" is then created. This `String` variable holds the contents of the `Array` variable that is passed to the function, and each element is separated from the next with an asterisk. The `for` loop cycles through "inputArray" until the length of that array is reached. For each index in the array (i.e., for each value of "i"), the corresponding element is added to the `String` variable "outputString," followed by an asterisk. That string is then sent out of the function.

```
function addAsterisksToArray(inputArray:Array)
:String
    {
        var outputString:String = new String;
        for (i = 0; i < inputArray.length; i++)
        {
            outputString += String(inputArray[i]);
```

```
outputString += "*";

    }

    return outputString;

}
```

In addition to defining this function, we also need to actually send our array to the function so that it can be turned into a string delimited with asterisks. The following code runs the array "responseArray" through the function "addAsterisksToArray" and appends the resulting string to your output variable:

```
    /*Send the array "responseArray" to the function
"addAsterisksToArray" and add the returned string
to the variable "output."*/

    output += addAsterisksToArray(responseArray);
```

To sum up, here are the steps you need to take to create usable output:

1) Create a new `String` variable that will store all your output in one long string.

2) At each point where you want to send something to output, append the contents of the relevant variable to your output variable using +=.

3) To make sure that there are no variable type incompatibilities, turn everything you add to the variable into a string first, for example, `String(condition)`.

4) After each piece of information you add to the output string, also add an asterisk using += "*" to delineate the information.

5) To output entire arrays, first send them to a function that will add asterisks between each element.

2. Creating an Excel Template for Data Output

Now that you have set up your output variable, you also need to create a template that will help you make sense of this output. The template consists of column headings that refer to each piece of information you have output in your data file. For instance, the first column might be labeled "subject," if you are outputting the subject number first. Your output template can be created in Excel; then, when you import your output into Excel, the data will fit the template. Here is what the beginning of your template might look like in Excel (Figure 9.2):

Figure 9.2.   Part of an Excel data output template.

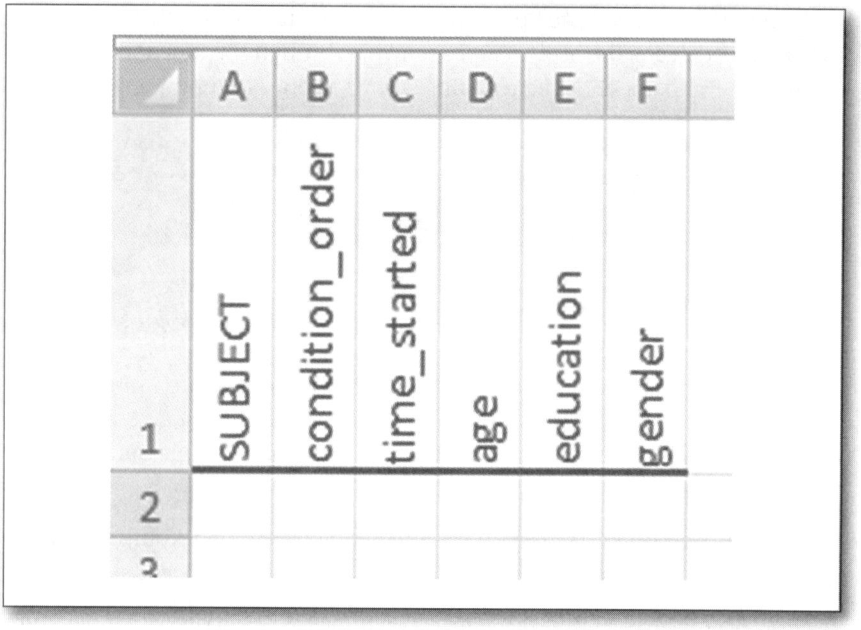

For variables that hold only a single piece of information (e.g., condition, gender, age, etc.), making a spot for them in the template is easy. The only thing you have to verify is that the order of the variables listed on the template is identical to the order in which information is added to your output variable.

When it comes to arrays, however, you have a few options as to the way you can output such information. Imagine you have a program where the user is presented with 10 questions in a random order, and for each question, the user provides an answer and a confidence rating. (Does this sound familiar? It should, because this was the exercise for "Chapter 6: Questionnaire Tools.") You need to output the following information for each question: the question itself or at least an index (so that you can identify the question), the response, and the confidence rating. Here is a matrix of the information for one user that you would like to send to your output (Table 9.1):

Table 9.1.	Sample data for 10 questions.		
Trial	*Question Index*	*Response*	*Confidence*
1	7	a	100
2	3	d	92
3	4	e	50
4	8	c	42
5	5	b	35
6	2	d	68
7	9	c	43
8	1	e	78
9	10	a	38
10	6	b	60

Here are two ways in which you could output this information in one string:

1) For each question, output the trial number, question index, response, and confidence rating sequentially; repeat for all remaining questions. Your output would look like this:

*1*7*a*100*2*3*d*92*3*4*e*50*4*8*c*42*5*5*b*35*6*2*d*68*7*9*c*43. . . etc.

And here is how it would look in your template (Figure 9.3):

Figure 9.3. Excel template with one line of output, showing data output by trial number.

	A	B	C	D	E	F	G	H	I	J	K	L	M	N	O	P	Q	R	S	T	U	V	W	X	Y	Z	AA	AB
	trial_number1	question_index 1	response1	confidence1	trial_number2	question_index2	response2	confidence2		question_index 2	response2	confidence2	trial_number3	question_index 3	response3	confidence3		question_index 3	response3	confidence3	trial_number4	question_index 4	response4	confidence4		question_index 4	response4	confidence4
1																												
2	1	7	a	100	2	3	d	92		4	e	50	4	8	c	42		5	b	35	6	2	d	68		9	c	43

2) You can output all the question indices in the order they appeared, followed by all the responses in the same order, and followed finally by all the confidence ratings in the same order. The advantage of this

method is that the responses and confidence ratings for each item in your study are in the same column for all participants. Your output would look like this:

*7*3*4*8*5*2*9*1*10*6*a*d*e*c*b*d*c*e*a*b*100*92*50*42 *35*68*43*78*38*60*

And here is how it would look in your template (Figure 9.4):

Figure 9.4. Excel template with one line of output, showing data output by variable.

A	B	C	D	E	F	G	H	I	J	K	L	M	N	O	P	Q	R	S	T	U
question_index1	question_index2	question_index2	question_index3	question_index3	question_index4	question_index4	response1	response2	response2	response3	response3	response4	response4	confidence1	confidence2	confidence2	confidence3	confidence3	confidence4	confidence4
7	3	4	8	5	2	9	a	d	e	c	b	d	c	100	92	50	42	35	68	43

The two methods described here are equally valid, and there are also many other ways you could output the data. You should play around with the options until you figure out which method is most intuitive and fits your purposes.

Note that in order to make the template work correctly, you need to make sure that all of the information is always added to the output variable in the same order, regardless of experimental condition or user input. If the data output is liable to differ by condition, you can adjust for this by inserting blanks where there is no information for a particular condition. Imagine the following scenario as an example of this: You have a survey that consists of 20 questions, but people in Condition A answer questions 1–15 and people in Condition B answer questions 5–20. If you append the answers to each of the 15 questions one by one to your output variable, you will have a string of 15 responses, but the first response for someone in Condition A will be to a different question than that of someone in Condition B. To correct for this, you could add five blanks to the beginning of the output for Condition B and five blanks to the end of the output for condition A. This will ensure that across both conditions, responses will line up in your template by question number. To add a blank to your output, simply append an asterisk without appending any data.

3. Testing the Output

In the next chapter, we cover how to put the program online and send your output variable to a text file that is also stored online. For now, even though you are not sending output to a text file, you can still test whether your output fits your template. Here is what you need to do:

1) After you have appended all the necessary information to your output variable, add a line of code that traces the output variable: `trace(output).`

2) When you test your program and get to the trace method you added as instructed earlier, the whole output string should appear in your Output window within Flash. Copy the output string and paste it into a new text document.

3) Open this text document in Excel. To locate the file, select **All files (*.*)** in the drop-down menu next to the File Name text field.

4) The Text Import Wizard will open up. Follow the instructions here for getting your data in the right format.

> In Step 1 of 3, for *Choose the file type that best describes your data,* select *Delimited* and click *Next.* In Step 2 of 3, you are required to indicate which symbols delimit your data. Under *Delimiters*, check *Other* and type an asterisk into the text field. At this point, you can click *Finish* and bypass Step 3 of the Text Import Wizard.

5) Now open up your template and paste your data underneath the headers. Check to see if all the data line up and make the relevant changes in your code and/or the template.

Exercise: For this exercise, you can use the program you created in the exercise at the end of "Chapter 6: Questionnaire Tools" and then edited in the exercise at the end of "Chapter 8: Using Timers and Recording Reaction Time." Now change the response format so that participants can type their response into an Input Text field. Create an output variable to store question index, answer, confidence, and reaction time for each question, and a template for this information. Try both methods, described earlier, for outputting array information.

In this chapter, you learned that there are two main alternatives for outputting your data: either after each trial, question, or section; or just once at the end of the program for each user. We focused on the second of these two options, but the principles you learned can be easily applied to the first. You learned that the most efficient way to gather all your information for output is to add each data point to a `String` variable. You learned how to delimit each separate data point in this string by interspersing asterisks after each one. You then learned how to make a template in Excel in order to be able to interpret the data output in this manner, and we warned you to make sure all your data line up with this template regardless of different conditions and different user behavior. Although you didn't learn how to actually send output to a text file (that comes in the next, and final, chapter), you used a workaround to copy the output from Flash and to view it in Excel to make sure it lines up with your template. These are all important things to do before you put your program online and allow other people to access it.

 ## Resources

The following links are hot-linked for your convenience at http://www.sagepub.com/weinstein.

http://help.adobe.com/en_US/AS2LCR/Flash_10.0/help.html?content= 00000335.html
A basic introduction to concatenating (adding together) Strings.

http://office.microsoft.com/en-us/excel-help/text-import-wizard-HP0101 02244.aspx
Introduction to the Text Import Wizard in Microsoft Office Excel.

CHAPTER 10

PUTTING YOUR
PROGRAM ONLINE

IN THIS CHAPTER, YOU WILL LEARN

- How to make sure your program is resistant to malfunctions and user mistakes
- Code for sending the output variable you created in the previous chapter to a text file
- That you need to upload four different files to your server in order for your program to be fully functional online
- About various things that can go wrong when you try to upload your program online

When you have finished writing your program and are ready to put it online, you will have to go through the following steps: (1) Make sure the program is airtight and there is no way an incompliant user can crash it by pushing keys at the wrong time, (2) add some code to your program to send out the output variable you created in the previous chapter to a text file, (3) "publish" the program to create an HTML page and Flash movie (.swf), and (4) upload a set of four files to your server.

To follow along with this chapter, you need to use a program you have created that includes an output variable (as specified in the previous chapter). Here you will learn how to get that program ready for the Web and how to send the data output variable you have created to a text file. This chapter assumes that you have your own web domain and hosting and know how to upload files to it. If you are not familiar with this, check the Resources section for some useful links.

1. Idiot-Proofing Your Program

The first thing you need to do before you put your program online is make sure that it is idiot-proof. To do this, imagine you are a very incompliant user, who does not follow instructions or press the right keys at the right time. Run through your program multiple times and try to press keys or click on the screen at times when you are not supposed to be interacting with the program. If you are not careful with your event listeners, unwanted events may be triggered. For instance, if you have a phase in your program where the user is passively watching the screen (e.g., in the study phase of an experiment), try pressing different keys to see if this affects the visual display. If any unwanted events are triggered, go back to your code and make sure all event listeners are removed when they are not needed.

You also want to ensure that users cannot inadvertently render your output unusable by typing certain characters or strings. For instance, double-check that the asterisk character (*) is restricted from input within your program if you intend to use this character as a delimiter between different responses in your output variable. Also, you may want to restrict the use of other characters or strings in order to minimize the chances that a nefarious user may manipulate your files. Programmers especially concerned with the security of their data may want to further investigate these issues.

2. Sending Output out of Flash

Now you need to figure out a way to send the output variable you created in the previous chapter to a text file. Unfortunately, Flash itself is not capable of doing this, so you need to write a script in another programming language (PHP) and some code in Flash telling it to run this script. The script will connect between Flash and the text file and transfer the contents of the output variable from one to the other. The PHP script itself is provided for you as a template (http://www. sagepub.com/weinstein), so you do not need to worry about writing that.

The code you need to add to your Flash program is in two parts. The first chunk of code sets up the method that will communicate with the PHP script. Here you indicate the exact location of your PHP script on the server. (We will upload the actual PHP script later and use the exact location of that script on your server in the code that follows.) You can add this code anywhere in the first Frame so that it is read when the program starts up.

```
var  varLoader:URLLoader = new URLLoader;

var  varURL:URLRequest = new URLRequest ("SERVER
ADDRESS OF YOUR PHP SCRIPT");

var submittedData:URLVariables = new URLVariables ();

varURL.data = submittedData;

varURL.method = URLRequestMethod.POST;
```

The explanation for how this code works is too advanced for this book, so all you need to know is that the text in quotation marks on the second line must be replaced with the location of your PHP script on your server and that the .POST method in the last line indicates that you will be sending information to the PHP script.

The second bit of code needs to be added to the program at the point where the output is ready to be transmitted. A good place to put this code would be right after the last piece of information is added to your output variable or when the user presses the last button—but make sure this is a button the user will definitely press, otherwise you will have no data output!

```
submittedData.inputData = output;

varLoader.load(varURL);
```

Recall that the variable that contains all our data (see the previous chapter) was called "output." Here we are sending this variable to the PHP script, which in turn will send it to the text file.

3. Publishing Your Program

Next you need to create the Flash movie and the HTML webpage that will hold the movie. The HTML webpage and Flash movie are created from within Adobe Flash by going to *File → Publish* (*Shift+F12*). This creates a template webpage (.html) file that you can edit to match the formatting of your website, and this template webpage will include all the code you need to display your Flash movie.

Various settings with regard to the size and quality of the webpage and the movie itself can be accessed under *File → Publish Settings* (*Ctrl+Shift+F12*). You can leave all the settings on default, except for disabling the movie menu. To do this, go to the HTML Settings tab and uncheck the box by Display Menu under Playback. This makes it impossible for the user who is accessing your program online to accidentally skip through to different Frames, which would cause difficulties with the program. If you leave the Display Menu box checked, the user can do this by right-clicking on the webpage and selecting Forward.

Once you have chosen your settings, simply select *File → Publish* (*Shift+F12*). The .html and .swf files will be created in the same directory as your .fla.

 ## 4. Uploading Your Program

To make your program fully functional online, you need to upload four different files: the HTML page, the Flash movie, a blank text file to store your output, and a PHP script file that will communicate between the Flash movie and the text file. Figure 10.1 illustrates the relationship among the files that will be on your server.

Figure 10.1. Diagram of the relationship among the files you need to upload. The Flash movie (.swf) is embedded in a webpage (.html). Once the program has come to the point where data needs to be output, a line in the code communicates with a PHP script. The PHP script in turn sends the data output to a text file.

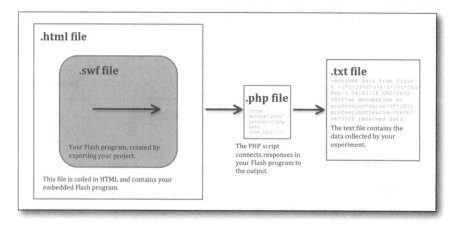

These are the four files you need to upload:

1) A basic webpage with your Flash "movie" (extension: .html) embedded—created when you published your program.

2) The Flash "movie" (extension: .swf)—created when you published your program.

3) A script that communicates between Flash and the text file to which you will output your data (extension: .php)—use the template provided.

4) A text file that will store your data (extension: .txt)—a new blank text file you create.

The first two files were created when you published your program in the previous step. Next you need the PHP document, which is a simple script. This script communicates with the Flash movie and receives the output variable, which is then sent to a text file. Rather than taking up a whole chapter with information about PHP, we have created a template for you to use. Go to http://www.sagepub.com/weinstein to download this document. If you use the exact code provided in Section 2 of this chapter and name the text file as specified here, all you need to do is upload this document to the same folder on your server as the other files required for running the program. If you decide to change the name of your text file, you need to edit the PHP script to match the name you are using. To edit a PHP script, open it in any text processing software and edit the relevant text, but make sure you save it with the extension .php.

Finally, you need a blank text file that will be referenced by the PHP script. This is where the output is sent. Create a new file in any text processing software (e.g., Notepad, Wordpad, or TextEdit), and save it with the name "myTextFile." Make sure the file you are saving has the extension ".txt" and the file name is exactly correct, otherwise the PHP script will not be able to send it the output.

5. Testing the Program and Troubleshooting

Now that your program is online, all that remains is to test it! Go to the HTML page in your browser. You should see your program, embedded in a webpage. Run through your program until the end, where it sends out the data. Now check your text file—you can either type in the location of the text file in your browser or download your text file from the server. A line of text should appear, beginning with "received from flash = 1" and followed by your data output.

Various things may go wrong with this process. Table 10.1 provides a quick troubleshooting guide:

Table 10.1.   Troubleshooting guide for online surveys and experiments.

Problem	Solution
The website does not load.	• Check to make sure you have the correct URL, and don't forget the ".html" extension.
The website loads but the movie is not embedded.	• Make sure you have Flash player installed on the computer you are using to access the website. Check to make sure that you uploaded the .swf document as well as the webpage.
There is no data output in the text file.	• Navigate to the URL of the PHP—the page that loads should be blank. If an error comes up on the page, there is a problem with the PHP template. • Make sure the text file is named to match the reference to it in the PHP script and that all four files are uploaded to the same directory on your server. Some servers do not allow PHP scripts. Contact the administrator of your server to verify this.

 ## 6. Wrapping Up

If you have reached this page, you've learned a lot of things about Flash! Hopefully, you are now ready to move on from the examples in the book to programming in Flash for your own research projects. But first take a minute to glance at the example program mentioned very early in the book (see "Why Flash?"). Go to http://www.sagepub.com/weinstein and click on the sample program. When you first looked at it, you probably had no idea how you would go about programming it yourself in Flash. Now you know all the techniques required to make this program, and more!

In this chapter, you learned that you really need to make sure your program is impossible to "break" by pressing the wrong key before you put the program online. You learned that Flash is not capable of sending output to a text file but can communicate with a PHP script to do so. You were given some code to add to your program for communicating with the PHP script and a template PHP script that does not need to be edited. You learned that there are four components to your online program: the HTML website; the swf, which contains your Flash movie; the php script; and a blank text file for collecting data. You learned about how to put these components together to make a fully functioning program that runs online and how to correct common errors. Good luck running your online surveys and experiments!

Resources

The following links are hot-linked for your convenience at http://www.sagepub.com/weinstein.

http://lifehacker.com/5683682/five-best-domain-name-registrars
A list of the five best domain registrars, as voted by a techy community.

http://filezilla-project.org/
The most popular free program for uploading files to a server.

http://www.lauraruel.com/j187/PDFs/flash_online.pdf
A journalist's guide to putting Flash programs online, which applies to experiments too.

http://adding-flash.blogspot.com/
How to put Flash content on a weblog or other website.

http://www.propublica.org/article/propublicas-guide-to-mechanical-turk
Overview of Amazon Mechanical Turk for those who want to have anonymous users complete their experiments.

http://net.tutsplus.com/tutorials/tools-and-tips/introduction-to-adobe-air/
An introduction to Adobe AIR, which provides another method of packaging an experiment.

RESOURCES INDEX

The following links are hot-linked for your convenience at http://www.sagepub.com/weinstein.

http://actionsnippet.com/?p=1640
　　A trick for making your randomly generated numbers more variable. ("Chapter 7: Condition Assignment and Randomization")

http://actionsnippet.com/?p=385
　　How to use the date stamp to automatically generate a unique Id for each user. ("Chapter 8: Using Timers and Recording Reaction Time")

http://adding-flash.blogspot.com/
　　How to put Flash content on a weblog or other website. ("Chapter 10: Putting Your Program Online")

http://as3-blog.net/?p=578
　　An advanced look at shuffling around the contents of an array. ("Chapter 7: Condition Assignment and Randomization")

http://blog.reyco1.com/method-of-removing-all-event-listeners/
　　A potential method of removing all event listeners. ("Chapter 3: Navigation")

http://coding.smashingmagazine.com/2011/01/11/keeping-web-users-safe-by-sanitizing-input-data/
　　The importance of sanitizing database input. ("Chapter 4: Working With Text and Keystrokes")

http://digitalmedia.oreilly.com/helpcenter/actionscript30cookbook/chapter1.html?page=6
　　Sample chapter from the ActionScript 3.0 Cookbook, explaining the switch statement. ("Chapter 7: Condition Assignment and Randomization")

http://edutechwiki.unige.ch/en/ActionScript_3_event_handling_tutorial #List_of_events
>   List of the most common Flash events. ("Chapter 3: Navigation")

http://filezilla-project.org/
>   The most popular free program for uploading files to a server. ("Chapter 10: Putting Your Program Online")

http://flash-creations.com/notes/actionscript_operators.php
>   Common mathematical operators in Flash. ("Chapter 2: ActionScript Basics")

http://gskinner.com/blog/archives/2010/07/some_thoughts_o.html
>   Some thoughts on TLF. ("Chapter 4: Working With Text and Keystrokes")

http://help.adobe.com/en_US/AS2LCR/Flash_10.0/help.html?content=000 00335.html
>   A basic introduction to concatenating (adding together) Strings. ("Chapter 9: Saving Data")

http://help.adobe.com/en_US/as3/dev/WS5b3ccc516d4fbf351e63e3d118a9b9 0204-7d01.html
>   Additional information on capturing keyboard input. ("Chapter 4: Working With Text and Keystrokes")

http://help.adobe.com/en_US/flash/cs/using/WS3e7c64e37a1d85e1e229110 db38dec34-7feba.html
>   Discusses the "code hinting" feature in Flash. ("Chapter 2: ActionScript Basics")

http://help.adobe.com/en_US/flash/cs/using/WSd60f23110762d6b883b18f10c b1fe1af6-7d29a.html#WSd60f23110762d6b883b18f10cb1fe1af6-7d22a
>   Setting Classic Text properties (including anti-aliasing options). ("Chapter 4: Working With Text and Keystrokes")

http://help.adobe.com/en_US/FlashPlatform/reference/actionscript/3/flash/ ui/Keyboard.html#constantSummary
>   Definitive list of constant keyCodes. ("Chapter 4: Working With Text and Keystrokes")

http://help.adobe.com/en_US/incopy/cs/using/WSa285fff53dea4f8617383751 001ea8cb3f-6e14a.html
>   An article about kerning. ("Chapter 4: Working With Text and Keystrokes")

http://home.earthlink.net/~craie/121/notes/vocabulary.html
Programming language vocabulary basics. ("Chapter 2: ActionScript Basics")

http://html-color-codes.com/
HTML color codes. ("Chapter 4: Working With Text and Keystrokes")

http://layersmagazine.com/build-a-simple-countdown-timer-in-flash.html
Creating a countdown timer in Flash. Includes more advanced design techniques as well as code samples. ("Chapter 8: Using Timers and Recording Reaction Time")

http://lifehacker.com/5683682/five-best-domain-name-registrars
A list of the five best domain registrars, as voted by a techy community. ("Chapter 10: Putting Your Program Online")

http://net.tutsplus.com/tutorials/tools-and-tips/introduction-to-adobe-air/
An introduction to Adobe AIR, which provides another method of packaging an experiment. ("Chapter 10: Putting Your Program Online")

http://office.microsoft.com/en-us/excel-help/text-import-wizard-HP01010
2244.aspx
Introduction to the Text Import Wizard in Microsoft Office Excel. ("Chapter 9: Saving Data")

http://snipplr.com/view/11307/as3-randomize-array/
Another method of randomizing the contents of an array. ("Chapter 7: Condition Assignment and Randomization")

http://tv.adobe.com/channel/how-to/
Adobe TV, which contains a series of useful how–to videos. ("Chapter 1: The Flash Interface")

http://www.actionscript.org/forums/showthread.php3?t=177515
A forum discussion of what precisely "void" means in functions. ("Chapter 2: ActionScript Basics")

http://www.actionscript.org/forums/showthread.php3?t=191468
A discussion thread about deselecting RadioButtons. ("Chapter 6: Questionnaire Tools")

http://www.actionscript.org/resources/articles/5/1/The-power-of-nested-
loops/Page1.html
Using "nested for loops" in Flash. ("Chapter 2: ActionScript Basics")

http://www.adobe.com/designcenter/flash/articles/flacs3it_astimeline_print
.html
A basic overview of how to use the Timer class. ("Chapter 8: Using Timers
and Recording Reaction Time")

http://www.adobe.com/devnet/flash/articles/flash_cs5_createfla.html
Another introduction to the Flash workspace. ("Chapter 1: The Flash
Interface")

http://www.adobe.com/devnet/flash/components.html
An exhaustive list of the component reference pages provided by Adobe.
("Chapter 6: Questionnaire Tools")

http://www.adobe.com/livedocs/flash/9.0/main/wwhelp/wwhimpl/common/
html/wwhelp.htm?context=LiveDocs_Parts&file=00000047.html
Flash data type reference. ("Chapter 2: ActionScript Basics")

http://help.adobe.com/en_US/FlashPlatform/reference/actionscript/3/Array
.html
The API entry for the Array object. ("Chapter 5: Presenting and Storing
Information in Arrays")

http://help.adobe.com/en_US/flash/cs/using/WSd60f23110762d6b883b18f10c
b1fe1af6-7f84a.html
A more detailed introduction to manipulating the Flash timeline.
("Chapter 3: Navigation")

http://www.designscripting.com/2010/08/html-tags-supported-by-flash/
List of HTML tags supported by Flash. ("Chapter 4: Working With Text
and Keystrokes")

http://www.flashandmath.com/howtos/eztimer/index.html
An advanced look at Timer performance, with a demonstration of the
error margin. ("Chapter 8: Using Timers and Recording Reaction Time")

http://www.flashcomponents.net/component/slider_component.html
Two implementations of the Slider component. ("Chapter 6: Questionnaire
Tools")

http://www.flashvalley.com/fv_articles/Naming_conventions_in_actionscript/
Some thoughts about naming conventions in Flash. ("Chapter 1: The
Flash Interface")

http://www.foundation-flash.com/tutorials/debugging/
Common errors people make in Flash and how to fix them. ("Chapter 2: ActionScript Basics")

http://www.gavilan.edu/csis/languages/comments.html
An interesting history of the use of comments in programming languages. ("Chapter 3: Navigation")

http://www.lauraruel.com/j187/PDFs/flash_online.pdf
A journalist's guide to putting Flash programs online, which applies to experiments too. ("Chapter 10: Putting Your Program Online")

http://www.macloo.com/examples/flash/button_states/
An illustration of the various Button states. ("Chapter 1: The Flash Interface")

http://www.onebyonedesign.com/tutorials/array_methods/
A list of advanced Array methods. ("Chapter 5: Presenting and Storing Information in Arrays")

http://www.propublica.org/article/propublicas-guide-to-mechanical-turk
Overview of Amazon Mechanical Turk for those who want to have anonymous users complete their experiments. ("Chapter 10: Putting Your Program Online")

http://www.republicofcode.com/tutorials/flash/as3arrays/
A simple introduction to Arrays. ("Chapter 5: Presenting and Storing Information in Arrays")

http://www.republicofcode.com/tutorials/flash/as3events/
Additional information on event handling. ("Chapter 3: Navigation")

http://www.signar.se/blog/as-3-charcodes/
charCode and keyCode reference. ("Chapter 4: Working With Text and Keystrokes")

http://www.smartwebby.com/Flash/external_data.asp
Loading data from external text files into Flash. Pair with Arrays to save lots of time. ("Chapter 5: Presenting and Storing Information in Arrays")

http://www.sunilb.com/programming/12-common-programming-mistakes-to-avoid
Common programming mistakes. ("Chapter 2: ActionScript Basics")

http://www.toxiclab.org/tutorial.asp?ID=69
    A tutorial for creating complex Buttons. ("Chapter 1: The Flash Interface")

http://www.ucl.ac.uk/~ucjtsre/B210.pdf
    Academic journal article measuring the accuracy of reaction time measurement in Flash. ("Chapter 8: Using Timers and Recording Reaction Time")

http://www.useit.com/alertbox/20040927.html
    A thorough discussion on when to use CheckBoxes versus RadioButtons. ("Chapter 6: Questionnaire Tools")

http://www.utexas.edu/learn/flash/buttons.html
    A tutorial about Buttons. ("Chapter 1: The Flash Interface")

http://www.video2brain.com/en/videos-699.htm
    A video introducing the Flash interface. ("Chapter 1: The Flash Interface")

http://www.w3.org/TR/html/
    General information on HTML. ("Chapter 4: Working With Text and Keystrokes")

http://www.webwasp.co.uk/tutorials/005/MX02/index.php
    A tutorial about Buttons. ("Chapter 1: The Flash Interface")

SUBJECT INDEX